THREE NUGGETS FROM THE RIVER OF LIFE

McDougal & Associates
Servants of Christ and Stewards of the
Mysteries of God

THREE NUGGETS FROM THE RIVER OF LIFE

HOW TO KNOW GOD FULLY, HOW TO RELATE TO HIS CHURCH, AND HOW TO WALK IN HIS PRESENCE

BY

KIM F. VOISIN

Published by:

McDougal & Associates
18896 Greenwell Springs Road
Greenwell Springs, LA 70739
www.thepublishedword.com

McDougal & Associates is an organization dedicated to the spreading the Gospel of the Lord Jesus Christ to as many people as possible in the shortest time possible.

ISBN: 978-1-950398-25-6

Printed on demand in the U.S., the U.K. and Australia
For Worldwide Distribution

Acknowledgments

I would like to give special thanks to the Holy Spirit, who teaches us all the things of Jesus Christ.

I would also like to thank Briggs Phariss for encouraging me to put into writing the things God had revealed to me over time. The seeds of the book were sown into my spirit on an oil platform in the Gulf of Mexico back in the 1980s. Spending many lengthy work weeks isolated there gave me wonderful opportunities at night when my shift was over to conduct Bible studies that were attended by as many as three hundred men. It was there that I first began sharing the nuggets you are about to explore.

I also want to thank my wife, Vanessa, and daughter, Brandy, for their hard work and invaluable input. They have supported and encouraged me throughout this endeavor.

Contents

Foreword by Joshua Mills

In your hand, you are holding a very special book. These pages were birthed through prophetic revelation, and the message they contain has the ability to change your life and open up new prophetic revelation for you, as you choose to embrace these *Three Nuggets from the River of Life.*

The fact that Pastor Kim has written a book about his revelations and the Word he finds to back them up is no surprise to me. Everything this man of God does is by revelation—from the founding of his amazing church, Vision Christian Center, in South Louisiana, to the day-to-day living of his own personal life. I have been blessed to be his friend, and I always look forward to every opportunity I have to fellowship with Kim and his wife, Vanessa, along with his family and church family, because they love God and their passion for His presence is contagious! They are always open and willing to let the Spirit do whatever it is He desires to do in their midst.

I am especially excited about this book because the very first time I ministered in Pastor Kim's church, I prophesied over him and told him that he needed to write a book! At the time, he didn't consider himself to be an author, and the thought of writing a book may have seemed far-fetched, but when God has a plan, He always makes a way.

A few years later, when I returned to minister at Pastor Kim's church, I received an email from my book editor, Harold McDougal (who lives in Baton Rouge, Louisiana), letting me know that he and his wife, Andrea, would be coming to join us in those special meetings. In that moment I knew that God's plan was beginning to unfold in a beautiful way. Over that weekend plans were made for the publishing of the book. God has a way.

I trust Pastor Kim's integrity and his sincere heart for the precious things of the Glory. Over the years, Pastor Kim has made it a habit to wait before the Lord each and every morning until

He knows what God wants him to do. Then he goes out and does it. No wonder he has been so blessed! My prayer is that you, too, would begin to know God in a more intimate way and that, as you read this book, the Holy Spirit would begin to illuminate your mind and spirit with His life-giving truths that come from Heaven. In this way, you may find yourself dipping your own hands into the River of Life and discovering supernatural nuggets of gold that God has made available for YOU.

I encourage every believer to read Pastor Kim's words, and then pray and study the Word for yourself and see what wonderful things the Spirit will bring to you. It is my great delight and honor to recommend that you read *Three Nuggets from the River of Life*. Once you start, you won't want to put it down.

Joshua Mills,
International speaker and bestselling author,
Moving in Glory Realms
www.joshuamills.com

Foreword by Jerry Stott

Dr. Kim Voisin is a practitioner, not just a theologian with great thoughts and ideas from years of ministry and study. I have personally experienced the constant outpouring that comes in like a flood upon every service where Dr. Voisin simply steps back and gives room for the Holy Spirit to have His way. I have witnessed services in thousands of churches, with multiplied thousands of leaders on almost every continent, and have only experienced this kind of open door in a few places on earth.

Dr. Voisin's revelations on entering into the presence of God and the outpouring of the Holy Spirit in every service have proven to me that "revivals" and "outpourings" are not just a once-in-a-lifetime hope for our churches, but can be experienced whenever and wherever the people of God gather.

The contents of this teaching bring us back to the beginning and to the understanding of what God's intention was. His Garden was there for mankind to draw in life and His presence every day, much like Enoch walked with God in body, soul, and spirit, and enjoyed that daily walk with his Creator.

I recommend this book for every believer who is desperate for the presence of the Holy Spirit to be in all and fill every part of their lives.

Jerry Stott, Ph.D.
South Pacific Region of Foursquare Churches
Author, Positioned for Miracles
Co-author, Positioned for the Gifts

Foreword by Wendy Nolasco

The transformative life of Kim Voisin is illustrated through the penned words of this book. His personal transformative experience turned into a powerful discipleship strategy for others is outlined so that any follower of Jesus desiring a deeper intimacy with Christ can follow. Kim is as genuine a man as he is a leader, and this work is the compilation of a life well lived and well led.

Wendy Nolasco
District Supervisor
MidSouth Foursquare District

God wants your total man prospering, above all.

3 John 1:2

Introduction

The three parts of this book represent three revelations given to me by God, and those three revelations deal with the progress of a person who decides to become a follower of Jesus Christ.

The first section, "The Total Redemption of Man," concerns what it means to accept Jesus as Lord and Savior of our lives and become a born-again Christian. As we will see, this redemption is not just for our soul, but for body, soul, and spirit. This brings a person into full fellowship with God.

The second section, "The Battle of the Fives," concerns how a new-born Christian should relate to the Church and the established ministries of the Church, what we often call the five-fold ministry, in order to stay free from sin, as well as grow and mature in the Christian faith. This brings a person into full relationship with the Church and enables them to begin operating in their individual calling.

The third section, "Life in the Garden," shows us how to live and walk in the Spirit so we can enjoy the very best God has to offer us. This enables a person to maintain their first love and to live in God's glory.

Taken together, the three revelations take us from salvation into growth, then to walking in God's presence day by day.

My whole life and ministry have revolved around revelations from God. As I have sought Him concerning each step of my Christian journey, He has revealed to me what I must do. I then went to the Scriptures and found the proof of what God was saying. And each revelation has taken me profoundly deeper.

These three particular revelations have been a blessing to me personally and to the members of the church I pastor in South Louisiana. I believe they will bless anyone who is hungry for more of God and will seek Him and study the teachings I present here, making them their own.

Kim F. Voisin
Bourg, Louisiana

Part I

The Total
Redemption of Man

Chapter 1

What Is the Total Redemption of Man?

This book reveals a depth of spiritual truth that is essential for these end-times. This revelation did not come from a collaboration of different studies (although I cherish spending time studying the Scriptures). It also didn't come from my own ability to understand scripture. Instead, this information came as pure revelation knowledge from the Holy Spirit. It came to me while I was praying one night, troubled in my spirit by the question of baptism.

This question had shaken me to the very core of my foundation, so I sat down and asked the Lord, "Help me to understand this subject." Even as I asked this question, the Holy Spirit began to come upon me and pour out revelation knowledge concerning baptism. He took me to various scriptures and showed me how this truth flows from Genesis to Revelation. He showed me how the whole focus of what Jesus and His apostles taught was to totally redeem man. Their message was centered on getting man totally and completely redeemed, to the place that you and I could be in position to walk in total fellowship with God.

WE ARE CALLED FOR FELLOWSHIP

God's Word says:

1 Corinthians 1:9
God is faithful, by whom ye were called unto the fellowship of His Son, Jesus Christ our Lord.

God is faithful, and He has called us, purchased us, redeemed us, and sanctified us to fellowship with Him. God has called us to a relationship with Him. His plan, from the very beginning, was to have a fellowship between us and Him.

When God created Adam, He created him unlike any other creature. It is said of Adam that

God created him *"in [His] likeness."* He was *like* God so that he could have fellowship *with* God.

I have a good beagle, a rabbit dog. My boys call him Buster because, they say, "He really busts those rabbits." Buster is a good hunter, but I can only relate to him as a hunting dog. I cannot fellowship with Buster because he was not created like me. He does not have the ability to reason, to think or to talk. He understands me only to the extent of his trained commands. In like manner, God did not create any other creature with which to fellowship, except man.

Before the fall of man, God came to the garden in the cool of the day to fellowship with Adam and Eve. That's why God made man just like Himself, with the same characteristics and traits. God wanted to fellowship with man on all three levels—body, soul, and spirit, a three-part man for a three-part God (Father, Son and Holy Spirit). Thus, a total fellowship could occur. This is the fellowship that existed in the Garden of Eden until Genesis 3. When man fell, all three parts of him fell. Therefore, man needs to be redeemed—body soul, and spirit.

To Be Totally Redeemed

The Gospel that Jesus, Paul, Peter, and John all preached was centered on getting the total man redeemed to fellowship with God. The very heart of this part of the book is to show that man was created for the purpose of having fellowship with God and that man must be totally redeemed to once again be in that position.

I can almost hear the reaction of some to what I'm saying here. "I've asked Jesus into my heart, and so I'm a redeemed man." Let me stop here and praise God that you are saved. Let me thank God that you have grown and matured to the level you are today. But I have a few questions to ask you: Do you walk with God like Adam did? Do you walk with God in the cool of the day and have Him impart revelation knowledge to you? If the answer is no, then you are not living a totally redeemed life.

As we have seen, 1 Corinthians 1:9 says that God has called us for fellowship. The truth is you can be saved and yet not totally redeemed. Being totally redeemed means going to the next level of experiencing Heaven, where we were meant to be all along.

Paul wrote to the Romans:

Romans 10:9-10

That if thou shalt confess with thy mouth the Lord Jesus, and shalt believe in thine heart that God hath raised him from the dead, thou shalt be saved.

But are we walking as sons and daughters of God?

WALKING AS A SON OR DAUGHTER OF GOD

We must learn how to walk as sons and daughters of God here on earth, just as Jesus did and said we should too. In fact, He said that we are gods, children of the Most High (see John 10:35). Paul also wrote:

Romans 8:19

For the earnest expectation of the creature waiteth for the manifestation of the sons of God.

Jesus said:

John 1:12

But as many as received him, to them gave He power to become the sons of God.

Many people misquote this scripture and say, "As many as believe on Jesus Christ become sons of God." The verse specifically says that He gave them POWER to become sons of God. The process is first asking Jesus Christ to come into your heart, confessing Him with your mouth, and believing in your heart that God has raised Him (Jesus) from the dead. At that point, you are qualified (meaning that you have the right) to be a son or daughter of God, but in order to obtain that right, you have to start acting like a child of God.

Jesus is our great example of how to do this. He was totally redeemed Himself, and we are going to see how to apply this to our lives in the next few pages. Come along and take this journey with me.

RIGHTLY DIVIDING THE WORD

In laying the foundation for this revelation, I believe it is necessary to take a closer look at the Scriptures:

John 3:16

For God so loved the world, that he gave his

only begotten Son, that whosoever believeth in
him should not perish, but have everlasting life.

Notice it does not say "shall not perish," but
"should not perish." We have heard it preached,
"shall not perish," but that's not what the Word
says. A more important example, as it relates to
this revelation, is found in Luke:

Luke 19:10
> *For the Son of man is come to seek and to save*
> *that which was lost.*

Many have preached this as though it says,
"to seek and to save the lost," but Jesus didn't
say here that He had come to seek and save the
lost. I'm not implying that He didn't, but this
particular scripture is saying much more than
that. What this verse says is *"that which was*
lost," which implies that He came to seek out
the thing which was lost, and the thing that was
lost was the full fellowship that man had with
God in the beginning of creation.

That's why Paul said, in 1 Corinthians 1:9, that
God is faithful, who has called us to fellowship.
To restore fellowship ... that's what Jesus came

to do. He brings us back into a full fellowship with God. So, in John 3:16, the Word is saying that if you believe on Him, you *should* not perish because He has given you everything you need—all the rights, privileges and characteristics of being a son of God. Now, it's up to you.

The message of "The Total Redemption of Man" is that you can walk out your life as a son of God. This section of the book will show you, through the teachings of the apostles, Jesus, and the Old Testament writers, how to live a life as God's son or daughter. If you can grasp this concept, it will help you not to be deceived by false prophets in these end days.

THE TEACHINGS OF THE APOSTLE PAUL

Let's take a look at the teachings of the apostle Paul, to see if we can find this same message there. He said to the Thessalonians:

1 Thessalonians 5:23

And the very God of peace sanctify you wholly; and I pray God your whole spirit and soul and body be preserved blameless unto the coming of our Lord Jesus Christ.

26

Paul was speaking to Christian believers to sanctify their whole being. He went on to identify the whole being as the spirit, the soul, and the body. I wonder why Paul would pray that born-again believers would have their whole being redeemed to God? It goes back to Genesis chapter 3, where all three parts of man fell.

Before that time, man had been very different:

Genesis 2:7

> *And the LORD God formed man of the dust of the ground, and breathed into his nostrils the breath of life; and man became a living soul.*

God made our body from dust and breathed into us the spirit (the breath of life), and we became a living soul.

PAUL'S THREE-PART GOSPEL

In Genesis 1:26, we see that God said, *"Let us make man in our image, after our likeness."* Therefore, we can look at man and see how God is.

Paul wrote to the believers in Corinth:

2 Corinthians 13:14

> *The grace of our Lord Jesus Christ, and the love of God, and communion of the Holy Spirit be with you all. Amen.*

Paul was teaching us to have a three-part relationship with God through the Son (Jesus Christ), the love of God the Father, and the Holy Spirit. Paul was saying that we have a body, a soul and a spirit that need sanctification in order to be preserved blameless to God the Father, God the Son, and God the Holy Spirit.

Man's soul is in direct correlation with God the Father. This part of man is his intelligence, his intellect and his knowledge, and it correlates to that part of the Godhead that all authority comes from. Remember, Jesus said He could do nothing except what He saw His Father do (see John 5:19).

Next, we see that the Spirit of man (the part of him that gives him life) is in direct correlation with the Spirit of God (the Holy Spirit). This is the part of God that hovered over the earth when He created it, the part that came over Mary and caused her to conceive Jesus.

Then, we see that the physical body of man is in direct correlation with the Son (Jesus). In

John 1:14, we read: *"the Word was made flesh and dwelt among us."* So we have a three-part God revealed as Father, Son, and Holy Spirit, who created a three-part man—body, soul, and spirit—so that He could fellowship with him.

Then, in Genesis 3, we see that man fell and lost his full, or total, relationship with God. Before the fall, man did not know shame. After the fall, he was ashamed and clothed himself with fig leaves and hid from the face of God. Later, we see man offering sacrifices to appease God because the fellowship with Him had been broken. Man had completely fallen–body, soul, and spirit–from his fellowship with the God of Creation.

Now, let us take a closer look at the apostle Paul's teachings. As we noted, in 2 Corinthians 13:14, he said, *"The grace of the Lord Jesus Christ* [one covenant], and the love of God [the second covenant], *and the communion of the Holy Spirit* [the third covenant] *be with you all."* Paul preached a three-part Gospel to redeem a three-part man.

Let's ask Paul how a three-part man can be redeemed. His answer is clear: through the GRACE of the Lord Jesus, through the LOVE of God the Father, and through the

COMMUNION of the Holy Spirit. This is our blueprint for walking in life as a son or daughter of God.

This is one of the biggest problems the Jews had. They saw the shift of focus from God the Father to Jesus, and this was hard for them to receive. So, thinking that they were doing God a favor, they tried to get the focus off of the Son (Jesus) and back on the Father (God). In the process, they missed what God had for them.

Some of us would say that was very foolish, and yet when Jesus (the Son) left the earth, He shifted the focus to the Holy Spirit, and still today, people are trying to shift the focus back to Jesus and away from the Spirit.

John 16:7 proves that Jesus shifted the focus to the Holy Spirit, when He said, *"It is expedient for you that I go away."* The word *expedient* here is translated from the Greek word *sumphero*, which means "to be better for, to be profitable for, or to be good for."

The reason Jesus shifted the focus to the Holy Spirit was that by this time only two parts of man had been redeemed. Through the Old Covenant, the soul had been redeemed (we will cover that in a later chapter), and through accepting and believing on Jesus Christ with water baptism, our body is redeemed. Now, Jesus said, "When He [the Holy Spirit] comes then you will receive all things."

Jesus was speaking about your spirit-man being redeemed, and that was not possible until the Day of Pentecost and what happened in the Upper Room that day. There, the focus shifted to the Holy Spirit, redeeming the third part of man, the human spirit.

Now we can understand why Jesus came to John to be baptized. John did not want to baptize Him and protested, *"I have need to be baptized of thee"* (Matthew 3:14). He was right about that. But Jesus answered him, *"Suffer [permit] it to be so now: for thus it becometh us to fulfill all righteousness"* (Matthew 3:15). Jesus did not need His flesh cleansed by baptism because He had no sin. He was simply fulfilling the sign of the covenant established by God. Because of this act, Jesus could walk on this earth as a totally redeemed man.

Immediately, Jesus was filled with the Spirit of God (see Matthew 3:16), and then He was led by the Spirit into the wilderness. Does that sound familiar? Paul wrote:

31

Romans 8:14

> *For as many as are led by the Spirit of God, they are the sons of God.*

THE TEACHINGS OF THE APOSTLE PETER

It is evident through scripture that Jesus, the apostles, and the Old Testament writers taught and preached the same message. Let's examine the teaching of the apostle Peter on this three-part Gospel:

1 Peter 1:2

> *Elect, according to the foreknowledge of God, the Father, through sanctification of the Spirit, unto obedience and sprinkling of the blood of Jesus Christ: Grace be unto you, and peace, be multiplied.*

Notice that the first thing Peter did here was to call upon the *"elect."* Then he said, *"according to"* and named three things that cause us to be the elect, the redeemed, the sanctified, the called, the saved. These three things are:

1). We are to have *"knowledge of God"* the Father. 2). We are to have it *"through sanctification of the Spirit,"* which is being filled with the Holy Spirit and having a relationship with Him. 3). We are to experience the "*sprinkling of the blood of Jesus Christ.*"

Peter was saying that in order to redeem your soul, you have to have knowledge of God the Father. Then, you must sanctify your spirit by being filled with the Holy Spirit, which sets you apart. Finally, you must be sprinkled with the blood of Jesus Christ, and that is our flesh being redeemed. This salvation comes by believing on Jesus and being baptized as an outward sign of the covenants. Here, Peter presents all three gospel points, just as Paul did.

In a later verse of the same chapter, Peter said:

1 Peter 1:18

Forasmuch as ye know that ye were not redeemed with corruptible things, like silver and gold, from your vain conversation received by traditions from your fathers.

You were redeemed by something more precious than gold. What was it?

1 Peter 1:19-20

But with the precious blood of Christ, as a lamb without blemish and without spot: who verily was

33

foreordained before the foundation of the world, but was manifest in these last times for you, who by him do believe in God, who raised him up from the dead and gave him glory; that your faith and hope might be in God.

This sounds a lot like Romans 10:9-10. Peter was showing us that the first part of our redemption is getting our sins cleansed, so we can establish a relationship with the soul and spirit. And you can't have a relationship between your soul and God until you get the body redeemed by the blood of Jesus. Likewise, you can't understand the Word of God until you get the Spirit of God in you.

Peter continued in verse 22:

Seeing that ye have purified your souls in obeying the truth.

Wait a minute! Peter was talking about another covenant here. He was talking about purifying your soul in obeying the truth. Earlier, he was talking about redeeming the flesh by the blood of Jesus. In Romans 10, we found that you were saved by accepting Jesus (believing that God raised Him from the dead). Paul said that with the heart man believes unto righteousness, and with the mouth confession is made unto salvation (see Romans 10:10). He didn't say anything about obeying anything or walking in anything. Why? Because that was just redeeming the flesh (getting Jesus in your heart).

Next, Peter explained redeeming the soul by having a relationship with the Holy Spirit:

1 Peter 1:23

Being born again, not of corruptible seed, but of incorruptible, by the word of God, which liveth and abideth for ever.

This scripture explains that the Holy Spirit works through the Word of God to redeem your soul.

THE TEACHINGS OF THE APOSTLE JOHN

Let's examine the writings of the apostle John to see if he speaks on this subject:

1 John 5:7

For there are three that bear record in heaven, the Father, the Word, and the Holy Ghost: and these three are one.

35

John has just identified the three parts of God—the Father, the Son, and the Holy Spirit. Verse 8 concludes:

And there are three that bear witness in earth, the Spirit, and the water, and the blood: and these three agree in one.

Here John shows three things that bear witness in the earth, which redeem man to the three parts of God. Let's look at each of these a little closer.

THE SPIRIT (HOLY SPIRIT)

In Verse 8, the word *Spirit* is referring to the Holy Spirit. Let's examine how the Holy Spirit bears witness with the human spirit. Acts 10:44-46 shows how Peter knew the household of Cornelius had received the Holy Spirit. He knew it because he *"heard them speak with tongues, and magnify God"* (verse 46). In other words, speaking in tongues (a spiritual language) and magnifying God was the outward sign that the household of Cornelius had their souls redeemed. This outward sign is how the

Holy Spirit bears witness that the human soul has been redeemed.

Notice that, in Acts 2:4, it was the Holy Spirit that gave the utterance when the hundred and twenty in the Upper Room were filled with the Holy Spirit and began to speak with other tongues.

AND THE WATER (JESUS)

John's next point was *"the water."* He was talking about baptism in water, which is a sign of the covenant between Jesus and man. In Galatians 3:27, baptizing in water is shown to be a sign that we are baptized into Christ. It is a sign, or a token, of the covenant between Jesus and man, which redeems or cleanses the flesh unto God through Jesus, His Son.

AND THE BLOOD (GOD THE FATHER)

When John mentioned *"the blood,"* he was speaking of circumcision. We know, from Genesis 17:9-14, that circumcision is a sign of the covenant between God the Father and man. Paul referred to circumcision as being *"that of the heart"*:

Romans 2:29

> *But he is a Jew, which is one inwardly; and circumcision is that of the heart, in the spirit, and not in the letter; whose praise is not of men, but of God.*

The Old Testament agrees:

Deuteronomy 10:16

> *Circumcise therefore the foreskin of your heart, and be no more stiffnecked.*

In Romans 4:9-12, Paul pointed out that Abraham received the sign of circumcision, which was the seal of the righteousness of his faith before he was ever circumcised in the flesh. So, then, Abraham is the father of all that believe, whether or not they were circumcised in their flesh.

THESE THREE AGREE IN ONE

Now there is a new thought before us. John said that these three signs *"agree in one."* Circumcision, baptism, and speaking in tongues are all the same, agreeing in one covenant. Just as you can't separate the Father, Son, and Holy Spirit, you cannot separate your body, soul, and spirit. These three things are a sign, or token, of the covenant between God and man.

Without applying all three parts of this covenant to yourself, you cannot be totally redeemed. But, by applying these three things, you can have a full relationship with God and walk in this life as His son or daughter.

As you can see, everywhere we turn in the Bible there is evidence of a three-part Gospel that redeems a three-part man.

JESUS THE SON OF GOD

Let's examine the teachings of Jesus Himself to see if we find this three-part Gospel:

Matthew 28:18-20

> *And Jesus came and spoke unto them, saying, All power is given unto me in heaven and in earth. Go ye therefore, and teach all nations, baptizing them in the name of the Father, and of the Son, and of the Holy Ghost: teaching them to observe all things whatsoever I have*

*commanded you: and, lo, I am with you always,
even to the end of the world. Amen.*

Mark 16:15-18

*And he said unto them, Go ye into all the world,
and preach the gospel to every creature. He that
believeth and is baptized shall be saved; but he
that believeth not shall be damned. And these
sign shall follow those that believe; In my name
shall they cast out devils; they shall speak with
new tongues; they shall take up serpents; and
if they drink any deadly thing, it shall not hurt
them; they shall lay hands on the sick, and they
shall recover.*

Notice the emphasis on believing the Gospel (or in Jesus) and being baptized as a sign of acceptance of that Gospel. There are certain signs that will follow those who believe, and these works will be done in the name of Jesus Christ. The mighty power of God is unleashed through the signs that follow those who believe and are baptized.

Jesus also told His followers to go out and teach the baptism in the name of the Father, the Son, and the Holy Ghost, telling them to observe the baptism of the Father (circumcision of the heart, to redeem the soul), the baptism of the Son (submersion in water, the sign of a redeemed flesh), and the baptism of the Holy Ghost (speaking in tongues, showing that the spirit of man is redeemed by the Spirit unto God).

Jesus has just commanded us to teach all nations the three baptisms, the covenants, or the three-part Gospel that God established to redeem a three-part man.

Chapter 2

The Redemption of Man's Soul: A Closer Look

How does man's soul become redeemed? First, we will need to establish exactly what man's soul is. *Webster's Dictionary* says that your soul is your "intellect and emotions."

Genesis 2:7

And the LORD God formed man of the dust of the ground, and breathed into his nostrils the breath of life; and man became a living soul.

God formed us from the dust of the ground (which is your body), he breathed into man the breath of life (which is your spirit), and, thus, we became a living soul. You're not a body, but you have a body. You're not a spirit, but you have a spirit. You are a living soul. That's what you are. Your intellect (what you think), your emotions (how you believe, how you feel about things) makes up your soul. Your soul is the part of you that experiences happiness, sadness or hurt. I've seen times where my soul was so happy it caused my physical body to run with excitement during worship. Let's take a minute to see just how the soul is redeemed.

How many of us want our mind (which is our ability to think, our emotions, and our ability to reason) redeemed? If your emotions are not redeemed, you cannot have fellowship with God. To explain this reasoning, think to yourself: can you get into your prayer closet while being really angry with someone and experience a total fellowship with God? It isn't possible because such things hinder you. You must first get the feelings out so that God can heal them. This, quite frankly, is the thing that hinders our fellowship with God the most: our thinking, our intellect, our knowledge.

Paul wrote:

1 Corinthians 8:1

Knowledge puffeth up, but charity [love] edifieth.

Our worldly wisdom tries to figure out God (which is not possible). Moses really knew God, and yet God told him, "The only thing you can see of Me is My back." Moses was the closest to God, but even Moses only saw God's back. We need to stop trying to figure out God or the moving of His Spirit and just receive all that He has for us.

CIRCUMCISION AS PART OF THE OLD TESTAMENT COVENANT

Genesis 17:9-14

And God said unto Abraham, Thou shall keep my covenant therefore, thou, and thy seed after thee in their generations. This is my covenant, which ye shall keep, between me and you and thy seed after thee; Every man child among you shall be circumcised. And ye shall circumcise the flesh of your foreskin; and it shall be a token [sign] of the covenant betwixt me and you. And he that is eight days old shall be circumcised among you, every man child in your generations, he that is born in the house, or bought with money of any stranger, which is not of thy seed, He that is born in thy house, and he that is bought with thy money, must need be circumcised: and my covenant shall be in your flesh for an everlasting covenant. And the uncircumcised man child whose flesh of his foreskin is not circumcised, that soul shall be cut off from his people; he hath broken my covenant.

We see, through these scriptures, that circumcision, under the Old Covenant, was required for anyone who adhered to the sign of this covenant between God and man. We also see that anyone who did not recognize this sign or do what God said to do was cut off from His people.

CIRCUMCISION IN THE OLD TESTAMENT (IN THE HEART)

Deuteronomy 10:15-16

Only the LORD had a delight in thy fathers to love them, and he chose their seed after them, even you above all people, as it is this day. Circumcise, therefore, the foreskin of your heart, and be no more stiffnecked.

In other words, circumcision was Israel's way of turning their hearts to God and not being stiffnecked toward Him or His ways. They chose not to walk in their own ways, but to start walking in His ways. When they were obedient and walked in God's ways, they circumcised the foreskin of their hearts.

Let's examine how this relates to baptism in water. Baptism in water is a physical sign, or token, of something that has already happened in your heart. So, in reality, baptism is something that happens in your heart. The three physical signs, or tokens, are circumcision, baptism, and tongues. They are only an outward show of something that has happened in the heart. When I start walking in the ways of God, my thinking, my intellect, and my emotions are redeemed unto God the Father, and I can now have fellowship with Him:

Jeremiah 4:3-4

> *For thus saith the LORD to the men of Judah and Jerusalem, Break up your fallow ground, and sow not among thorns. Circumcise yourselves to the LORD, and take away the foreskins of your heart, ye men of Judah and inhabitants of Jerusalem: lest my fury come forth like fire, and burn that none can quench it, because of the evil of your doings.*

Jeremiah was saying for us to break up the hard, shallow and flaky ground that you are trying to sow into. This ground is not good for planting. He correlated this with the heart. He was saying that circumcision is getting all the flaky stuff out of you. For example, that could include bad habits, bad ideas, bad beliefs, or whatever else you are holding on to that just doesn't line up with the Word of God. Get the ground of your heart broken up and prepared, so that you can receive the Word of God into it. This ground must be capable of developing good, stable roots in God. Our hearts will change, and we will no longer be stiffnecked toward God.

Remember the Parable of the Sower in Matthew 13 (see verses 3-9 and 18-23)? This parable shows us the only seed (Word of God) that can bring forth fruit (results) is seed that falls on good ground. Jesus was showing how important it is to have good ground in our hearts. The way we accomplish getting good ground is to be circumcised in our hearts.

It is evident, in the writings of Deuteronomy and Jeremiah, that the sign of the covenant of circumcision was really intended and expected to be in the heart and not just a physical sign in the flesh.

47

CIRCUMCISION UNDER
THE NEW COVENANT
(IN THE HEART)

Paul wrote:

Colossians 2:8-15

Beware lest any man spoil you through philosophy and vain deceit, after the tradition of men, after the rudiments of the world, and not after Christ. For in him dwelleth all the fullness of the Godhead bodily. And ye are complete in him, which is the head of all principality and power: in whom also ye are circumcised with the circumcision made without hands, in putting off the body of the sins of the flesh by the circumcision of Christ: buried with him in baptism, wherein also ye are risen with him through the faith of the operation of God, who hath raised him from the dead.

And you, being dead in your sins and the uncircumcision of your flesh, hath he quickened together with him, having forgiven you all trespasses; blotting out the handwriting of ordinances that was against us, which was contrary to us, and took it out of the way, nailing it to his cross; and having spoiled principalities and powers, He made a show of them openly, triumphing over them in it.

There is a circumcision made without hands, and here we see an emphasis on getting away from the sin of the flesh. In doing that, we become circumcised with Christ. We find redemption for our soul (heart) when we refrain from sin. And, in obedience to the Word, we ask Jesus into our hearts and bury the old man of sin in baptism.

Romans 2:29 also speaks of circumcision being of the heart. Paul also wrote:

Romans 4:7-12

Blessed are they whose iniquities are forgiven, and whose sins are covered. Blessed is the man to whom the Lord will not impute sin.

Cometh this blessedness then upon the circumcision only, or upon the uncircumcision also? for we say that faith was reckoned to Abraham for righteousness. How was it then reckoned? when he was in circumcision, or in uncircumcision? Not in circumcision, but in uncircumcision. And he receive the sign of circumcision, a seal of the righteousness of the faith which he had yet being uncircumcised: that he might be the father of all them that believe, though they be not circumcised; that righteousness might be imputed unto them also: and the father of circumcision to them who are not of the circumcision only, but who also walk in the steps of that faith of our father Abraham, which he had being yet uncircumcised.

Here the apostle Paul was saying, "Blessed is the man whose sin is not imputed (assigned or credited) to him because he is righteous by faith." Notice that these scriptures show how Abraham received righteousness. It was imputed unto him before he was circumcised in the flesh, which shows that circumcision was only a sign of the righteousness that came to him by faith. This proves that when we walk by faith, we circumcise the heart.

So far, we have seen two ways to be circumcised in the heart: 1) Putting off the old man, the body of sin, and 2) Walking by faith.

WALKING BY FAITH

Abraham is a classic example of walking by faith. He was a rich man when God spoke to him to leave his family and go to a land He would show him (see Genesis 12:1). God promised to make Abraham a great nation, to bless him, and make his name great. Abraham believed God and trusted Him. Therefore, he left his riches and set out on a journey that exposed him to all the rigors of traveling (living in tents, being confronted by thieves, robbers, and bandits, not knowing where he was going, etc.). Extreme uncertainty is easily seen in this situation, but Abraham set out on this journey for only one reason: God had told him to do it.

Abraham believed God and was obedient to what God had told him to do, and his believing and obeying were counted unto him as righteousness. He is a great example of a person with absolute faith.

What is faith? Faith is stepping out and doing something when everything in the physical realm says you can't. It's when the devil is screaming in your ear, and yet you step up and obey anyway. When you operate like this, you are circumcising your heart. This is because you are not walking in your own intellect, but by faith in God.

Let's see what the Scriptures have to say about faith:

Romans 10:17

> *So then faith cometh by hearing, and hearing by the word of God.*

In this verse, the Greek word translated as *word* is *rhema,* meaning "an utterance." An utterance from God means that He speaks to you. This gives you confidence:

1 John 5:14-15

> *And this is the confidence that we have in him, that, if we ask any thing according to his will, he heareth us: and if we know that he hears us, whatsoever we ask, we know that we have the petitions that we desired of him.*

Romans 10:17 expresses the fact that we can have faith when God says we can have it, because faith comes by hearing the utterance of God. Faith does not come when your spouse or friend says you can have it; faith comes by hearing the utterance of God.

When we put Romans 10:17 and 1 John 5:14-15 together, they say this: Faith comes when you hear God and know that God has heard you. Your soul is redeemed when you hear from God and know that God has heard you. This is fellowship—a two-way relationship with God. When we develop this two-way relationship with Him, our prayer life can mature. It will go from submitting petitions to getting instructions on how to fix our specific problems. So let's look at how to develop such a relationship, or fellowship, with God.

To illustrate this scripture in action, I have a short story from a pastor. The pastor was driving down the road praying, "Oh, God, whatever it takes, I want to know You." Then he pulled a piece of gum out of his pocket, opened it, and started to throw the wrapper out the car window.

Just then, the Holy Spirit said, "Don't throw that wrapper out!"

The pastor proceeded to throw the wrapper out anyway, but a mile down the road he suddenly realized that the Holy Spirit had left him. He stopped the car and asked, "Holy Spirit, what happened?"

The Holy Spirit said, "I told you not to throw that paper out the window. Now, if you want to know Me, go back and pick it up."

Today this pastor will tell you, "If you ever see me in the churchyard picking up paper, I'm just getting to know Jesus better."

Here we can clearly see that if we are to walk in faith, develop a relationship and have communication with the Holy Spirit, we need to start doing the small things we feel impressed to do. If you work on the small things first, eventually you will notice you are growing in this area and can move on to greater things:

1 Peter 1:18-23

> *Forasmuch as ye know that ye were not redeemed with corruptible things, like silver and gold, from your vain conversation received by tradition from your fathers; but with the precious blood of Christ, as of a lamb without blemish and without spot: who verily was foreordained before the foundation of the world, but was manifest in these last times for you, who by him do believe in God, who raised him up from the dead and gave him glory; that your faith and hope might be in God.*
>
> *Seeing that ye have purified your souls in obeying the truth through the Spirit unto unfeigned love of the brethren, see that ye love one another with a pure heart fervently; being born again, not of corruptible seed, but of incorruptible, by the word of God, which liveth and abideth for ever.*

The first thing Peter talked about here was our flesh already being redeemed unto God. He said that we were redeemed by the precious blood of Christ. We have identified the covenant of baptism in water, which results in the redemption of the flesh. Peter went on to say that our faith and hope are in God, and we believe in God because of Jesus. How did Jesus cause us to believe in God? We believe because we know that God raised Jesus from the dead and gave Him glory. Here, Peter is talking about us having a foreknowledge of God that results in the redemption of the soul.

Next, Peter says that we have purified our souls in obeying the truth through the Spirit. Then he says we are born again by the Word of God, that incorruptible seed. Here is evidence of a third way to get our soul redeemed, by being born again by the Word of God, which lives and abides forever.

In summary, we have established three ways of having the soul redeemed unto God. These three will often flow together or overlap in effect, but the end result is your soul being redeemed unto God. The first was putting off the old man of sin, or being circumcised in your heart. We found in the Old Testament that circumcision was not only in the flesh, but men were expected to circumcise their hearts toward God. We've also discovered that being circumcised in the heart was exactly what the apostles taught and preached in the New Testament. This circumcision of the heart redeemed man's soul to God the Father.

Second, we found that walking by faith redeemed man's soul unto God. Abraham was counted to be righteous because he believed God and walked according to what God told him. Thus, walking by faith redeemed Abraham's soul unto God the Father.

Third, we found that man's soul was redeemed by the Word of God, the incorruptible seed. Man is born again by the Word of God, which is the soul being redeemed unto God.

Chapter 3

The Redemption of Man's Body

Now, let's talk about how the body of flesh is redeemed. We presented an overview of the total redemption of man in Chapter 1. In chapter 2, we talked in somewhat greater detail about the redemption of man's soul unto God the Father. Now, we will go into greater detail on the redeeming of the body of flesh unto Jesus:

Romans 7:18-25

For I know that in me (that is, in my flesh,) dwelleth no good thing: for to will is present with me; but how to perform that which is good I find not. For the good that I would I do not: but the evil which I would not, that I do. Now if I do that I would not, it is no more I that do it, but sin that dwelleth in me. I find then a law, that, when I would do good, evil is present with me. For I delight in the law of God after the inward man: but I see another law in my members, warring against the law of my mind, and bringing me into captivity to the law of sin which is in my members. O wretched man that I am! who shall deliver me from the body of this death? I thank God through Jesus Christ our Lord. So then with the mind I myself serve the law of God; but with the flesh, the law of sin.

The first declaration in this passage is: *"no good thing"* dwells in the flesh. In other words, our flesh is the part of us that wants to sin. Our spirit longs to worship God, but, in verse 23, we see the flesh warring against the the soul, our mind, or emotions.

Let's see if we can clarify what is happening here. We have had our soul redeemed, but the flesh wars, or fights, against the soul. Paul was saying that no matter how much we grow or mature in the Lord, our flesh will always want to sin.

What can deliver us from this bad situation, or, as Paul said, *"the body of this death"*? He answered, in verse 25, *"I thank God through Jesus*

Christ our Lord." He has just said how he would get the body of flesh redeemed. It is *"through Jesus Christ our Lord."* We redeem our flesh when we go to Jesus Christ.

Today, in the Body of Christ, we have a problem with people not having their flesh redeemed. This is because people have turned to religion instead of turning to Jesus. We get into bondage when we start relating to our religious affiliations: "I'm a Catholic," "I'm a Baptist," "I'm an Assembly of God," etc. The bondage comes because the flesh is not redeemed, and it wars against the soul (mind), bringing the soul into captivity. Paul said it in 2 Corinthians 3:6: *"the letter killeth, but the Spirit giveth life."* If we try to walk by the letter, relating to our religious persuasion, expecting to get strength to walk through this life from our church traditions or religious beliefs, we will fail. There is only one thing that redeems us from this body of death, and that is Jesus Christ.

The first thing we need to do is get our eyes off of "my church teaches this," or "this is the way we believe," and get our eyes on having a relationship with Jesus Christ. The only way we can have fellowship with God is to have our flesh redeemed, because God cannot look upon sin. Jesus became flesh so that He could take our sin upon Himself. Now, we can have fellowship with God, and Jesus can relate to us because He became flesh. This is why Jesus is the Mediator between God and man (see 1 Timothy 2:5).

Let's take a moment to talk about how we put the flesh down:

Romans 6:1-7

What shall we say then? Shall we continue in sin, that grace may abound? God forbid. How shall we, that are dead to sin, live any longer therein? Know ye not, that so many of us as were baptized into Jesus Christ were baptized into his death? Therefore we are buried with him by baptism into death: that like as Christ was raised up from the dead by the glory of the Father, even so we also should walk in newness of life.

For if we have been planted together in the likeness of his death, we shall be also in the likeness of his resurrection: knowing this, that our old man is crucified with him, that the body of sin might be destroyed, that henceforth we should not serve sin. For he that is dead is freed from sin.

The apostle Paul was telling us here that the body of sin is destroyed (freed) by baptism into Jesus:

Galatians 3:27

For as many of you as have been baptized into Christ have put on Christ.

This is saying to us that when we are baptized into Jesus, we are baptized into His death. Even as Christ was raised from the dead, we will walk in newness of life. Our old person (how we used to act) is put to death, even as Jesus was put to death, so that our sinful flesh might be destroyed.

Notice that the Word does not say we are baptized into a particular church denomination, the Father or the Holy Spirit. We are baptized into Jesus. In the book of Acts, every scripture that identifies how a person was baptized says that they were baptized *"in the name of Jesus."* Why? Because baptism in the name of Jesus redeems our body of flesh unto Jesus Christ. It is a covenant between man and Jesus. It is by having a relationship with Jesus that we are set free from sin.

The only thing that will get you out of condemnation is a relationship with Jesus. You can have every man of God on this side of Heaven pray with you, but guilt will not leave. Guilt will never leave until you have a relationship with Jesus and seal the covenant with Him by being baptized into Jesus Christ.

It is clearly seen in the Scriptures that total submersion in water, the symbol of being buried with Jesus, is a necessary requirement for baptism. The water does not save you; it is the act of obedience to the sign, or token, of the covenant that we must follow. Just as with the Old Testament covenant of being circumcised, we found that having the foreskin cut off did not suffice. A circumcision of the heart was necessary. Now we see that our hearts must be baptized.

Galatians 3:27 tells us that when we are baptized, we put on Jesus and are baptized to fulfill the sign of the covenant. Jesus had no sin. He did not need the flesh cleansed. But, since He was walking as a man, He was obedient to fulfill this sign, or token, of the covenant established by God the Father:

1 Peter 3:20-22

> *Which sometime were disobedient, when once the longsuffering of God waited in the days of Noah, while the ark was a preparing, wherein few, that is eight souls, were saved by water. The like figure whereunto even baptism doth also now save us (not the putting away of the filth of the flesh, but the answer of a good conscience toward God,) by the resurrection of Jesus Christ. Who is gone into heaven, and is on the right hand of God; angels and authorities and powers being made subject unto him.*

Here, the experience of Noah was likened unto a baptism. That will be more important to us later on. The main point we need to see here is that baptism does not save us. Notice also that the emphasis is on the good conscience toward God that saves us and not the putting away of the filth of the flesh by going under the water. It is the obedience to the sign of the covenant and having a good conscience toward God that is important.

In 1 Corinthians 10:1-4, the people following Moses were said to have been *"baptized unto Moses"* (verse 2) because they were under the cloud and in the sea. Remember, God led the children of Israel by a cloud in the daytime (see Exodus 13:21-22), and they passed through the sea (see Exodus 14:22). Saying that they were following the cloud signified that they were obedient to God, and we just established in Chapter 2 that obedience toward God results in the circumcision of the heart, which redeems man's soul to God. Here, we see that the New Testament calls this a baptism. Luke 3:16 shows us that being filled with the Holy Spirit is also called a baptism.

The sign of the first covenant, redemption of the soul, is circumcision of the heart. The sign of the second covenant, redemption of the flesh, is baptism in water by full submersion in the name of Jesus. The sign of the third covenant, which was the redemption of the human spirit, is baptism in the Holy Spirit.

Webster's Dictionary defines *baptism* as "the induction or the initial experience of anything." For example, a soldier's first exposure to gunfire is called "a baptism in fire." We need to broaden our thinking concerning the word *baptism*.

Until the Holy Spirit gave me this revelation knowledge on the total redemption of man, the first and only thing that came to my mind when I heard the word *baptism* was submersion in water. After studying the Bible, I now clearly think of all three covenants.

Now, let's look at the age-old question: Why did the disciples baptize in the name of Jesus? Earlier in this chapter, we saw that the book of Acts tells us to baptize *"in the name of Jesus."* If you go back to all the scriptures and look up the word *name*, it is *onomah* in the Greek, which means "name, title." It does not mean "authority." There is an argument that the "name of Jesus" was used to signify the authority of Jesus, but that's not correct because every usage of the word "name" means "title" in the Greek.

Baptism in the name of the Father, Son, and Holy Spirit came into being in 325 A.D. and was brought about by the Church Council of Nicea. The first question that comes to mind is simply this: if this baptism was started in 325 A.D., doesn't it show us that a change took place? And if baptism was changed, that means the apostles did not baptize that way, right?

Another side of the baptism question is that Jesus said in Matthew 28:19 to baptize in the name of the Father, Son, and Holy Spirit.

Because Jesus did say that, we have half of the Christian world baptizing in the name of the Father, Son and Holy Spirit and believing in the Trinity, or three-part God. The Trinity is right, but their baptism is wrong. The apostles baptized in the name of Jesus.

Then we have the other half of the Christian world baptizing in the name of Jesus, which is right, but they are teaching that there is no Father, Son and Holy Spirit. Their teachings put all three as one being, and that is wrong.

So what we have now is the whole Christian world "goofed up" over this one subject. I can't understand how the devil could use something as simple as baptism to get the Christian world into such division. This is serious, and we need to resolve it.

Let's take a look at the half that only baptize in the name of Jesus. Why are they doing this? They know that baptism in the name of the Father, Son, and Holy Spirit started in 325 A.D. and have concluded that it could not be right (and it wasn't). Because of this, they throw out the concept of the three-part God redeeming a three-part man. But the only way they can explain what Jesus said in Matthew 28:19 is to conclude that He filled three offices at one time. That is not what He said.

In order to promote this teaching, we would have to tear out certain parts of our Bible, because they do not line up with only baptizing in the name of Jesus. For example, we have to throw out the baptism of Jesus at the Jordan River where the Father spoke from Heaven. Jesus was on the Earth, and the Holy Spirit came upon Him as a dove.

On the other hand, if we insist on only baptizing in the name of the Father, Son, and Holy Spirit, we have to tear out all the places in Acts where the apostles baptized in the name of Jesus. God's Word was inspired by the Holy Spirit (see 2 Timothy 3:16 and 2 Peter 1:21). Therefore, who are we to take such liberty with it, practicing a cafeteria religion of "take what you want?" God wants us to profit from the entirety of the Word of God. We are to seek out the whole counsel of God:

2 Timothy 2:15

Study to shew thyself approved unto God, a workman that needeth not be ashamed, rightly dividing the word of truth.

What I am saying is that it is necessary for the heart to have a full transformation. If you were baptized as a sign of accepting Jesus, which is a good thing, I would ask you to add a heart transformation so that you may go on unto perfection.

Throughout my Christian life, I have talked to both sides about the information they each believe, and I came away needing a better answer. There is too much in the Word of God that disproves both of them, which is how this book was birthed.

A Better Answer

Everything in the Bible is the Holy Spirit's better answer. We have already established that the covenant with the Father is called a baptism, the covenant with the Son is called a baptism, and the covenant with the Holy Spirit is called a baptism. To clearly see this better answer, let's go to the Scriptures where Jesus talked about baptism (see Matthew 28:18-20 and Mark 16:15-18).

Let me point out that these two references are sister chapters, which means they are both talking about the same event. However, we see Matthew focusing on what Jesus said to *"teach,"* and Mark focusing on Jesus telling them to *"preach the gospel."* The effects of preaching *"the gospel"* Mark wrote of was people believing, baptizing, and doing all sorts of signs, wonders, and miracles in the name of Jesus. Mark focused on the effects of the Gospel on the individual— getting the flesh redeemed and walking in the power of God.

When we accept Jesus, we are accepting the Gospel. When we get baptized, it's as a sign, or token, of having accepted the Gospel of Jesus Christ. We have accepted who Jesus is. Therefore, we are baptized in His name and do all the signs Mark wrote about in Jesus' name. If we are not doing those signs, we might need to check what we were baptized into or what we believe in.

Let me tell you something in all humility: if you believe the Gospel that Jesus Christ preached, if you have accepted and are walking in the Gospel that the apostles preached, that same Gospel they got from Jesus, then these signs will follow you. You will cast out devils, you will lay hands on the sick and see them recover.

Mark emphasized the effects of preaching the Gospel: believing, baptism and signs. We also see that the power of God literally explodes when the Gospel is preached.

Next, let us go to Matthew's account. This passage, when compared to the account given in Mark 16, has probably caused more controversy in the Body of Christ than any other scripture:

Matthew 28:18-20

And Jesus came and spake unto them, saying, All power is given unto me in heaven and in earth. Go ye therefore, and teach all nations, baptizing them in the name of the Father, and of the Son, and of the Holy Ghost: teaching them to observe all things whatsoever I have commanded you: and, lo, I am with you always, even unto the end of the world. Amen.

Let us examine exactly what Jesus said here. He said, *"Go ye therefore, and teach all nations."* In Mark, Jesus said *"preach the gospel."* In Matthew, He was focused on what the Gospel is, not the results, or effects of the Gospel being preached.

Then Jesus went on to say exactly what the Gospel is that you should teach: *"Baptizing them in the name of the Father, and of the Son, and of the Holy Ghost."*

BAPTIZING IN THE NAME OF THE FATHER

Now you can see why so much emphasis and explanation has been placed on baptism earlier in the book. It seems that the whole church world has missed what Jesus said here. If we baptize **in the name of the Father**, it must equate to, or be, the exact same thing as the **baptism of the Father.** We have already established that the baptism of the Father is circumcision.

In Deuteronomy and Jeremiah, considering the whole counsel of God, the Word revealed that circumcision was not just the cutting off of the foreskin of the man child on the eighth day. God told them to be circumcised in their heart.

BAPTIZING IN THE NAME OF THE SON

Jesus also said, *"Baptizing them in the name ... of the Son."* Here, baptizing **in the name of the Son** would be the exact same thing as the

baptism of the Son. The baptism of the Son is full submersion in water. This signifies being buried with Jesus, which results in the redemption of the body of flesh.

BAPTIZING IN THE NAME OF THE HOLY SPIRIT

The final thing that Jesus said to teach all nations was **baptism in the name of the Holy Ghost**. In like manner, as with the Father and the Son, baptizing in the name of the Holy Spirit is the exact same thing as the **baptism of the Holy Spirit**. Here I will simply point out that the baptism of the Holy Spirit redeems our human spirit unto God. This will be covered in greater detail in Chapter Four.

Let's review what we have learned so far: Jesus said to teach all nations three baptisms. Let's remember the definition of baptism, "the initial induction or experience of something." The first one is the baptism of the Father, which is circumcision of the heart toward God, resulting in the redemption of man's soul. The second one is the baptism of the Son, which is submersion in water in the name of Jesus, resulting in our body of flesh being redeemed unto God.

The third one is the baptism of the Holy Ghost, which is man being filled with the Holy Ghost (with the sign of speaking in tongues), resulting in man's human spirit being redeemed unto God.

Jesus said to teach others about these three baptisms or the three covenants between God and man. He wants us to teach people about a three-part God that created a three-part man for fellowship. We are to teach them about the three seals to God's three-part covenant in the earth.

Now we can start to see how complete God's salvation plan is. I think you will agree with me on this point. This is a better answer than having to tear out, or ignore, parts of the Bible where we see a three-part God or where we see baptism in the name of Jesus.

In verse 20, Jesus concluded by saying, *"Teaching them to observe all things whatsoever I have commanded you."* What things would Jesus like us to observe? Well, the things He just spoke about:

- The Baptism of the Father
- The Baptism of the Son
- The Baptism of the Holy Ghost

This one point is very important. If the things we believe cause us to tear out, skip over, or simply ignore verses in the Bible to justify our beliefs, we are wrong.

Chapter 4

The Redemption of the Spirit

In this final chapter of Part I, we will talk about the redemption of the human spirit, the part that was breathed into us by our Creator, the part that longs to praise and worship God.

John 16:12-16

I have yet many things to say unto you, but ye cannot bear them now. Howbeit when he, the Spirit of truth, is come, he will guide you into all truth: for he shall not speak of himself; but whatsoever he shall hear, that shall he speak: and he will show you things to come. He shall glorify me: for he shall receive of mine, and shall show it unto you. All things that the Father hath are mine: therefore said I, that he shall take of mine, and shall show it unto you. A

*little while, and ye shall not see me: and again,
a little while, and ye shall see me, because I go
to the Father.*

Let's take a look at verse 12. *"I have yet many things to say unto you, but ye cannot bear them now."* We need to realize that Jesus was speaking to the apostles when He said this. He was speaking to the men who had walked with Him, living with Him for some three years, sitting under His teachings, hearing His parables, and seeing the many signs, wonders, and miracles which He did. And yet He told them, "There are many things I want to tell you that you can't yet receive."

Jesus went on, in verse 13, to say, *"Howbeit when he, the Spirit of truth, is come, he will guide you into all truth: for he shall not speak of himself; but whatsoever he shall hear, that shall he speak."* What Jesus was saying here is that there are some things we cannot understand unless we understand them through the Spirit of God. We can only get a certain level of understanding of the Word of God in our soul or in our intellect. We can only understand it to a certain extent. Yes, we can understand the Word of God enough to be saved, but there are some deeper things in God that are only revealed by the Spirit of God. In this chapter, as we continue to talk about the redemption of the human spirit, you will begin to realize that it's not until the human spirit is redeemed that one can begin to walk in the supernatural realm, the Spirit realm of God, and understand things which are only seen in the Spirit.

"When the Holy Spirit comes, He'll show you the things of Jesus." Jesus was telling the apostles that, in their current status, or condition, they could not receive spiritual things. Their soul was redeemed, and they had knowledge of God. Their flesh was redeemed, and they had been baptized. But their spirits were not yet redeemed because they had not yet been filled with the Holy Spirit. And, because their spirits were not yet redeemed, they could not bear, or receive, the many things Jesus had to say.

The reason the disciples could not bear these things was that such things are spiritually discerned. It was only after being redeemed by the Spirit that they could receive spiritual things. You see, the Spirit of God speaks directly to your spirit, and it is only through this relationship that one can receive revelation.

So far, we have learned that the soul is redeemed by the Word of God, by walking in faith, and adhering to the things of God. The flesh is redeemed by accepting the Gospel of Jesus Christ and entering into the covenant of baptism. At this point, you have a certain relationship with the Father and the Son. You call yourself a Christian and walk in the things of God to a certain degree. But when it comes to spiritual things, you just cannot seem to understand them. When it comes to visions and dreams, seeing angels, or casting out devils, you seem not to be able to step into it. The problem is the human spirit not yet being matured in the things of God.

This next set of scriptures reveals that when the Holy Spirit comes, you will begin to see the things of God:

1 Corinthians 2:9-16

> *But as it is written, Eye hath not seen, nor ear heard, neither have entered into the heart of man, the things which God hath prepared for them that love him. But God hath revealed them unto us by his Spirit: for the Spirit searcheth all*

things, yea, the deep things of God. For what man knoweth the things of a man, save the spirit of man which is in him? even so the things of God knoweth no man, but the Spirit of God.

Now we have received, not the spirit of the world, but the Spirit which is of God; that we might know the things that are freely given to us of God. Which things also we speak, not in the words which man's wisdom teacheth, but which the Holy Ghost teacheth; comparing spiritual things with spiritual. But the natural man receiveth not the things of the Spirit of God: for they are foolishness unto him: neither can he know them, because they are spiritually discerned. But he that is spiritual judgeth all things, yet he himself is judged of no man. For who hath known the mind of the Lord, that he may instruct him? but we have the mind of Christ.

There are several points I want to bring out from this passage concerning the redemption of the human spirit. Verse 9 says, "Eye has not seen, ear has not heard, and it has not entered into the heart of man those things that God has prepared for those that love him." Jesus was saying that the natural man cannot receive the things of the Spirit. There is no way we can perceive in the natural realm (seeing, hearing, or understanding in our intellect) those things that God has prepared for us. We (within our soul, our intellect, our ability to think and reason) cannot imagine the greatness and fullness of the Kingdom of God.

In recent years, the Body of Christ has been blessed with an abundance of good teaching on who we are, what we are, and what is ours in Christ. It should be settled in our spirit that He is our Provider, Healer, and Protector, and He desires to speak to us. But even if we know, understand, and apply all the healing, prosperity, and confession messages, we still cannot imagine what great things God has prepared for us. This is because certain things can only be seen in the Spirit realm through the Spirit of God.

If we stopped at verse 9, we would think that one just cannot know all the things of God. But, when we go on to verse 10, we understand that God reveals them to us by His Spirit. *"For the Spirit searcheth all things, yea the deep things of God."* The Spirit of God reveals the deep, meditated revelation, or *rhema* word, from the teaching of the *logos* or written Word of God.

When we go into the Spirit of God, we begin to communicate with the Spirit of God. This is when we begin to read the Bible, and things begin to come alive to us. They become *rhema*, "an utterance from God." Suddenly, the Holy Spirit opens the Scriptures, and we can see clearly how they apply to our own situation. Faith begins to soar, as the deep plan of God is revealed, which will redeem and deliver.

Just reading the Bible will give a certain level of understanding, but the same words can come alive by the Spirit of God. We begin to see the impact of how the Scriptures can be applied. Suddenly they are no longer stories written on a page, but a love letter from God, speaking directly to you and me.

God is concerned about every need and every situation of our lives.

Hebrews 6:1-3

> *Therefore, leaving the principles of the doctrine of Christ, let us go on unto perfection; not laying again the foundation of repentance from dead works, and faith toward God, of the*

doctrine of baptisms, and of laying on of hands, and of resurrection of the dead, and of eternal judgment. And this will we do, if God permit.

Here, the writer of Hebrews tells us that once we have our foundation established in God, we don't have to lay it all over again. He says, *"Let us go on unto perfection."* In 1 Corinthians 3:10-14, it is clear that what we build our foundation on is what we will be judged on, which will determine if we receive a reward. If we are to go on to perfection, we must get into the deeper things of God. And the only way to get into the deeper things of God is through the Holy Spirit. The only way to receive revelation through the Holy Spirit is by having our human spirits redeemed.

Looking back at 1 Corinthians 2:14, we see that the natural mind cannot understand the things of God. They are foolish to the natural mind because they are spiritually discerned. Have you ever tried to tell someone who is not saved about the deep things of God? As simple as it is to you, they cannot understand or receive it. This is because the things of God are spiritually discerned. If we argue and debate the deep things of God, we err, because people need salvation first. Then their soul will be redeemed, and they can begin to receive the deep things of God. It is okay to witness, but not to debate the hidden truths or deep things of God. It is the spiritual man who discerns all the things of God. By the Spirit, he can begin to look into the deeper things of God.

PRAYING IN THE HOLY SPIRIT

Jude tells us:

Jude 1:20

> *But ye, beloved, building up yourselves on your most holy faith, praying in the Holy Ghost.*

Praying in the Holy Spirit, praying in the Spirit of God, builds up our faith. By the end of this chapter, we will begin to realize why this is true. If praying in the Holy Spirit builds up my faith, I need to understand exactly what it is:

Acts 10:44-48

> *While Peter yet spoke these words, the Holy Ghost fell on all them who heard the word. And*

they of the circumcision which believed were astonished, as many as came with Peter, because that on the Gentiles also was poured out the gift of the Holy Ghost. For they heard them speak with tongues, and magnify God. Then answered Peter, Can any man forbid water, that these should not be baptized, which have received the Holy Ghost as well as we? And he commanded them to be baptized in the name of the Lord. Then prayed they him to tarry certain days.

Peter was preaching the Word of God to the household of Cornelius, and their souls were redeemed by the Word. Verse 44 says that they received the Holy Spirit while Peter was still preaching. In verse 46, we see how they knew the spirit of those of the household of Cornelius had been redeemed when they received the Holy Spirit. It says *"They heard them speak with tongues, and magnified God."* Those who had come with Peter were astonished that the gift of the Holy Spirit was poured out upon the Gentiles.

We have just identified, in this scriptural setting, the three-fold redemption of man we are writing about. First, they heard the Word of

God, and their souls were redeemed. Second, they were filled with the Holy Spirit, and their human spirits were redeemed. Third, Peter commanded them to be baptized in the name of the Lord, which redeemed their flesh.

It is interesting to note, in Acts 11, that Peter was confronted in Jerusalem by those of the circumcision (probably converted Pharisees, see Acts 15:5), who were condemning him for going to the Gentiles and eating with them. To justify his actions, Peter simply reviewed the whole matter from Joppa to where the Holy Spirit had fallen on the Gentiles in the house of Cornelius (see Acts 11:2-18).

Peter ended his review by saying that he re-membered how the Lord had said, *"John indeed baptized with water; but ye shall be baptized with the Holy Ghost"* (verse 16). Peter pointed out, in verse 17, that God had given the Gentiles the Holy Spirit, just like the Jews had received it at the beginning. He concluded by saying, *"What was I, that I could withstand God?"* (same verse). When they heard that, the people who had condemned Peter held their peace and glorified God saying, *"Then hath God also to the Gentiles granted repentance unto life"* (verse 18).

How did these people know that the Holy Spirit had fallen on the household of Cornelius, and God had given the Gentiles repentance unto life? It was because they recognized the redemption of the human spirit, when the Holy Spirit fell on them, and they spoke in tongues.

Notice what Paul said to the Ephesian believers:

Ephesians 4:30

> *And grieve not the Holy Spirit of God, whereby ye are sealed unto the day of redemption.*

The household of Cornelius had been sealed by the Holy Spirit.

SPEAKING IN TONGUES, THE LANGUAGE OF THE HOLY SPIRIT

Speaking in tongues is the language of the Spirit:

1 Corinthians 13:1

> *Though I speak with the tongues of men and of angels, and have not charity [love], I am become as sounding brass, or a tinkling cymbal.*

The focus of this entire thirteenth chapter of 1 Corinthians is love. It shows us the absolute necessity for all the gifts of the Holy Spirit to operate out of love. In fact, it shows us that whatever we do, if we do not do it out of love, it profits us nothing.

But Paul reveals more than this great truth at this particular point in his writing. Here Paul reveals that he spoke in two languages. He said that he not only spoke in his normal language (the tongues of men), but he went on to say that he spoke *"with the tongues ... of angels."* What is the language of the angels?

In Hebrews 1:14, we find that angels are ministering spirits. This makes me think that since they are spirits, they must speak a spiritual language. Paul said that he thanked God he spoke with tongues *"more than ye all"* (1 Corinthians 14:18). Jesus said, in John 4:24, *"God is a spirit: and they that worship him must worship him in spirit and in truth."* We can have a certain level of communication with God in our natural language, and a certain level of communication with Him when our soul is redeemed. We can have an even deeper level when our flesh is redeemed, but the deepest level of communication with

God comes when our spirit is redeemed unto God by the Holy Spirit, through talking to God in His own language.

To have this ultimate level of fellowship, or communication, with God, we must operate in the Spirit realm:

1 Corinthians 14:2

For he that speaketh in an unknown tongue speaketh not unto man, but unto God.

This scripture reveals that speaking in tongues is direct communication with God in His language. This gives us more understanding of what Jude meant when he said, *"Building up yourselves on your most holy faith, praying in the Holy Ghost"* (Jude 20). How does praying in the Holy Spirit build up my faith? First, let us realize that praying in the Spirit is a one-on-one communication between our spirit and the Spirit of God. God is a spirit. If we want to communicate with Him, we have to do it in His language. I'm not saying God doesn't speak English. What I *am* saying is that we have a scriptural foundation for speaking in tongues or praying in the Spirit.

We learned earlier that faith comes when we hear from God (see Romans 10:17), and we know that God has heard us (see 1 John 5:14-15). When we pray in the language of the Spirit, we know that He hears because we are talking to Him in His language. As our spirit is moved by His Spirit, He is able to convey to us things that cannot even be expressed in words (see Romans 8:26). We discovered earlier, in Romans 10:17, that this is how faith comes. This brings us back to Jude 20 and shows us why Jude said to build up our faith, praying in the Holy Ghost.

After all this, I think we can better understand what Jesus meant when He said that we must worship God *"in spirit and in truth."* Now we can clearly understand Peter's writings, in Acts 11, when he reminded us of what Jesus said about knowing they were baptized in the Holy Ghost, when he heard them speak in tongues.

Romans 8 gives us an even deeper understanding of what we are talking about, the redemption of the human spirit unto the Spirit of God:

Romans 8:26-27

Likewise, the spirit also helpeth our infirmities: for we know not what we should pray for as we ought: but the Spirit itself maketh intercession for us with groanings which cannot be uttered. And he that searcheth the hearts knoweth what is the mind of the Spirit, because he maketh intercession for the saints according to the will of God.

The first thing this verse says is that we don't know what we should pray for. In my maturing, I remember praying for my wife, children, parents, cousins, friends, relatives, jobs, and health. Finally, it got down to the cat, dog, and gold fish. Suddenly, it seemed as though I had completely run out of things to pray for. It also seemed as though I had worn myself and God out with prayer. I was just kidding with the animals, but you get my point.

The Holy Spirit knows that our knowledge is limited when we pray for people and situations. Therefore, through groans that cannot be uttered, He helps us by praying through us. Praying in the Spirit allows us to pray with effectiveness and wisdom we don't have within ourselves (our soul or intellect). If you will search your own heart after praying in the Holy Spirit, you will know what you are praying for.

Verse 27 indicates that you will be praying for the saints in the perfect will of God. This scripture is evidence of a one-on-one relation-ship between your spirit and the Spirit of God, resulting in effective prayer.

Now we can begin to understand what Paul meant when he prayed, in 2 Corinthians 13:14, that the communion of the Holy Spirit be with you. We need this type of communion with God. It only comes when our spirit is redeemed and we have a relationship with the Holy Spirit.

Now, let us examine the first sermon preached after the outpouring of the Holy Ghost on the Day of Pentecost. In Acts 2, Peter preached from verse 14 through verse 36. We see in verse 37 that after the people heard the Word of God (which redeemed their soul), they were pricked in their hearts and asked what they should do. Here, we see the three-fold redemption of man.

First, Peter preached the Word of God to them (which redeems man's soul); second, they re-ceived the Word of God, it brought conviction, and they wanted to know what they should do. In this very first altar call, Peter instructed them: *"Repent, and be baptized ... in the name of Jesus Christ for the remission of sins"* (verse 38). Then Peter added, *"And ye shall receive the gift of the Holy Ghost"* (same verse). The Word redeemed their soul, accepting Jesus redeemed their flesh, and the receiving of the Holy Spirit redeemed their human spirit.

Let us dwell a moment on this gift of the Holy Spirit that Peter talked about here. In verse 39, Peter said, *"For the promise is unto you, and to your children, and to all that are afar off, even as many as the Lord, our God, shall call."* When he said, *"The promise is unto you,"* he was speaking of Jews who were hearing that sermon. When he said, *"The promise is ... to your children,"* he was speaking of future generations of Jews. When he said *"the promise was ... unto all that are afar off, even as many as the Lord our God shall call,"* he was speaking of the Gentiles. In this light, let us examine ourselves a moment. Has the Lord God called you? If He has, the promise of the gift of the Holy Spirit is for you. Have you been drawn to Jesus? Remember, Jesus said, *"No man can come to me, except the Father which hath sent me draw him"* (John 6:44). So, if you come to God, the promise of the Holy Spirit is yours.

We, as individuals, can stop at any point we want to, in this three-fold redemption of man. God will not force us. My heart's desire is for you to receive the words of this book and become a fully redeemed person, in full fellowship with God. It is my deepest desire for you to be in full harmony and fellowship with the total God—God the Father, God the Son, and God the Holy Spirit.

When we see this happening on a large scale in the Body of Christ, then I believe we will see that great outpouring of the Holy Spirit that has been prophesied as "the latter rain." That is the same latter rain that will precede the coming of our Lord and Savior, Jesus Christ.

Part II

The Battle of the Five

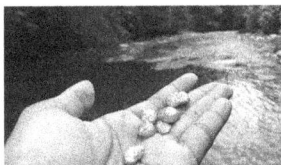

Chapter 5

What Is the Battle of the Five?

As I noted in the introduction, this is the second of the three revelations in this book. It concerns how a new-born Christian should relate to the Church and the established ministries of the Church, in order to stay free from sin, and to grow and mature in the Christian faith. When a person is in full relationship with the Church, it enables them to begin operating in their individual calling.

Let me lay the foundation of how this particular revelation came to me. I was seeking the Father about things that were going on in my own personal life. The Holy Spirit had instructed me several months before to build a church that would be for teens. As I began to build that church, it seemed as if the powers of Hell broke loose over me. When I sought God about it, the Father spoke to me through the Spirit, saying that five evil spirits had been assigned to me by Satan, to stop the church we had begun.

As I meditated on what the Holy Spirit had spoken, I asked Him, "What are the names of the evil spirits, and what are their methods of attack?"

The Holy Spirit began to tell me the names of these spirits and their avenues of attack against me. One evil spirit would be a religious spirit that would use the religious forces of the area to try to destroy the work. The second spirit would come against my mind and emotions. The third spirit would fight my finances and mechanical things, to put pressure on my family life. The fourth spirit would be a spirit of false words and signs. The Holy Spirit informed me to be very careful and watch this particular spirit closely. This is a very dangerous spirit. The last spirit would be sickness. It would do its best to afflict my family.

The Holy Spirit instructed me to address these five spirits directly and not give them place. He said to bind them in the name of Jesus and to go forward. That is exactly what I did.

Let me clarify: each of our assignments from God is different. Each area has spirits that will hinder the work and assignments of God. The ones I have identified are the ones assigned to try to hinder me and the work God gave me to do. You will hear from God yourself, if you are to identify a spirit by name and to bind him.

As I meditated on these five avenues of attack, the Holy Spirit said to me, "This is the fivefold ministry of Satan." This was a term I had never heard before.

I said to the Holy Spirit, "I know the fivefold ministry of God found in Ephesians":

Ephesians 4:11-12

And he gave some, apostles; and some, prophets; and some, evangelists; and some, pastors and teachers; for the perfecting of the saints, for the work of the ministry, for the edifying of the body of Christ:

I said, "If there is a fivefold ministry of Satan, You will have to show me a scripture that lists it. It also has to be in the same level of authority—the first being equal to an apostle, the second being equal to a prophet, and so on."

The Holy Spirit brought me to Ephesians 6:

Ephesians 6:10-12

Finally, my brethren, be strong in the Lord, and in the power of his might. Put on the whole armour of God, that ye may be able to stand against the wiles of the devil. For we wrestle not against flesh and blood, but against principalities, against powers, against the rulers of the darkness of this world, against spiritual wickedness in high places.

There it was: Satan, principalities, powers, ruler of the darkness in this world, and spiritual wickedness in high places. He had brought me to the structure of the fivefold ministries of Satan.

In this second section of the book, I will show you how God has the fivefold ministry structure He uses to move in this world. I will also show you how Satan has a counterfeit structure to fight against the Church.

First, we must lay a foundation. Let's answer some questions that are probably in your mind by now. Why is the fivefold ministry of God listed by the name of the office and the fivefold ministry of Satan listed by the spirit behind the office? For clarity sake, I will list several important points. For the natural mind's sake, I will bring out scriptures of the different offices and their counterfeits.

First of all, Satan is not the Holy Spirit and does not have the same power as the Holy Spirit. The Holy Spirit is God; therefore He can be all places, knowing all things at all times. This allows Him to be the spiritual force behind all the fivefold offices of God. Satan, on the other hand, is nothing more than a fallen angel. He has to work through a structure, to govern, or rule over, his kingdom:

Ephesians 3:8-11

> *Unto me, who am less than the least of all saints, is this grace given, that I should preach among the Gentiles the unsearchable riches of Christ; and to make all men see what is the fellowship of the mystery, which from the beginning of the world hath been hid in God, who created all things by Jesus Christ: to the intent that now unto the principalities and powers in heavenly places might be known by the church the manifold wisdom of God, according to the*

eternal purpose which he purposed in Christ Jesus our Lord.

Principalities and powers were known to the Church as the *"manifold wisdom of God"* (Ephesians 3:10) and God's *"eternal purpose ... in Christ Jesus our Lord"* (verse 11). Satan has no principalities of his own, so he can only copy what he sees the Church doing.

What is the purpose of the fivefold ministry of God? Again, let us look to Ephesians:

Ephesians 4:11-13

> *And he gave some, apostles; and some, prophets; and some, evangelists; and some, pastors and teachers; for the perfecting of the saints, for the work of the ministry, for the edifying of the body of Christ: till we all come in the unity of the faith, and of the knowledge of the Son of God, unto a perfect man, unto the measure of the stature of the fullness of Christ.*

So, these ministries are:

- For the perfecting of the saints
- For the work of the ministry

- For the edification of the Body of Christ
- To bring the unity of the faith
- To bring us to that perfect man and the fullness of the measure of Christ

If you are not submitted to the fivefold ministry of Christ, you will never become the perfect man or woman God wants you to be. You cannot get out on your own, away from the Body of Christ. That is when you will be deceived. (We will get into more detail on this point, as we teach on the different offices.)

What is the purpose of the fivefold ministry of Satan?

Ephesians 6:11-12

Put on the whole armor of God, that ye may be able to stand against the wiles of the devil. For we wrestle not against flesh and blood, but against principalities, against powers, against the rulers of the darkness of this world, against spiritual wickedness in high places.

It is evident that the purpose of the fivefold ministry of Satan is to fight against and tear down the Body of Christ. It also serves as a means by which Satan governs his kingdom.

Please take time to read and study these scripture verses, as you go through the book. Study them so they will become rooted in you. Just to read what I have discovered in God's Word is not enough; you must see it for yourself and allow the Holy Spirit to make it alive to you.

As we have seen, Paul wrote to the Corinthian believers that the natural mind cannot receive the things of God:

1 Corinthians 2:14-16

But the natural man receiveth not the things of the Spirit of God: for they are foolishness unto him: neither can he know them, because they are spiritually discerned. But he that is spiritual judgeth all things, yet he himself is judged of no man. For who hath known the mind of the Lord, that he may instruct him? but we have the mind of Christ.

Paul wrote to the Romans that *"to be carnally minded is death"*:

Romans 8:5-6

For they that are after the flesh do mind the things of the flesh; but they that are after the Spirit the things of the Spirit. For to be carnally minded is death; but to be spiritually minded is life and peace.

Your natural mind does not want you to understand the fivefold ministry of God or for you to flow with these ministries. It also does not want you to understand the fivefold ministry of Satan or how to fight against it.

Please take a moment and pray for the leading of the Holy Spirit before you go on. This is vital to your understanding.

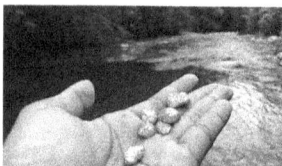

Chapter 6

The Apostle

Now, let us begin to examine each of the offices of the fivefold ministry of God. First, we will look at the apostle:

Ephesians 2:19-22

Now therefore ye are no more strangers and foreigners, but fellowcitizens with the saints, and of the household of God; and are built upon the foundation of the apostles and prophets, Jesus Christ himself being the chief corner stone; in whom all the building fitly framed together groweth unto an holy temple in the Lord: in whom ye also are builded together for an habitation of God through the Spirit.

Take special note of the following:

- In verse 20, we are built on the foundation of the apostles and prophets.
- In verse 21, we are fitly framed together growing unto a holy temple in the Lord.
- In verse 22, we are a habitation of God.

THE APOSTLES OF GOD

We can see that apostles and prophets work hand in hand to lay a foundation for the Body of Christ. The problem in many churches today is that they are not allowing the apostles and prophets to lay a foundation for what the church is doing. They readily accept the pastor, evangelist, and teacher, but are afraid of the apostles and prophets. We must submit to the entire fivefold ministry of God, not just the part we want, if we are to be that perfect man in full stature of the measure of Christ.

Let's look at it again:

Ephesians 4:11-13

And he gave some, apostles; and some, prophets; and some, evangelists; and some, pastors and teachers; for the perfecting of the saints, for the work of the ministry, for the edifying of the body of Christ: till we all come in the unity of the faith, and of the knowledge of the Son of God, unto a perfect man, unto the measure of the stature of the fullness of Christ.

LAYING THE FOUNDATION

How does an apostle of God lay a foundation for the Body of Christ? Paul wrote:

1 Corinthians 9:1-2

Am I not an apostle? am I not free? have I not seen Jesus Christ our Lord? are not ye my work in the Lord? If I be not an apostle unto others, yet doubtless I am to you: for the seal of mine apostleship are ye in the Lord.

The seal of Paul's apostleship was that he had founded the church at Corinth in the Lord. He had taught them what the Word of God said and how it applied to them. He had raised them up in the things of God. Everything the church at Corinth taught and believed they had learned from him. As we read the book of 1 Corinthians, notice how Paul corrects them concerning their wrong beliefs, and wrong actions, and how he revealed to them the mysteries of God:

2 Corinthians 4:1-2

Therefore seeing we have this ministry, as we have received mercy, we faint not; but have renounced the hidden things of dishonesty, not walking in craftiness, nor handling the word of God deceitfully; but by manifestation of the truth commending ourselves to every man's conscience in the sight of God.

Here we see the apostolic ministry of Paul laying the foundation in the Word for the Church. It is the apostle's job to lay a foundation for what the Body of Christ believes and teaches in the Word. The apostles are the pacesetters in the doctrine that is accepted in the Body. These are men and women of God widely respected for their doctrinal stand. A good example would be Martin Luther, who taught, "The just shall live by faith." Some apostles have awakened the Body of Christ to the truth that God is our healer and healing is a today gift. These great leaders have set the standards for what the Word is saying to the Church today.

THE APOSTLES OF SATAN

Where are the false apostles found in the Scriptures? Remember the earlier conversation I had with God about the authoritative structure of Satan having to be listed in the same order as the fivefold ministry of God. Satan's authoritative structure can be identified in the 11th and 12th verses of Ephesians 6. Satan is listed first in verse 11. Therefore, Satan has to be the spirit behind the false apostle. Through the false apostle, Satan fights against the office of the apostle. Let's look to the Scriptures to see if that is true.

SATAN FIGHTING THE APOSTLE

Let's go back to 2 Corinthians 4 and read a little further:

2 Corinthians 4:3-4

But if our gospel be hid, it is hid to them that are lost: in whom the god of this world hath blinded the minds of them which believe not, lest the light of the glorious gospel of Christ, who is the image of God, should shine unto them.

110

In these verses, Paul is saying that he laid a foundation in the Word, but that the god of this world blinded the minds of them that were lost. Here, Satan himself was fighting and stopping man from seeing what the apostle of God was doing.

Again, Satan is not God, and he cannot be all places at one time. Therefore, Satan must set up an authoritative structure whereby he governs, or directs, his leaders (or false apostles). They, in turn, govern the lower levels of satanic authority.

Satan's realm is like our United States Army. The President, as Commander in Chief, does not counsel with the privates or even the sergeants. He counsels with the generals. They tell him what the lower levels need in order to accomplish their job. Satan's army operates in the same way. He counsels with his false apostles, and they tell him what the lower satanic levels need to accomplish their job.

Just how does Satan blind those who are lost, so that they don't hear the teachings of the true apostles?

2 Corinthians 11:13-14
For such are false apostles, deceitful workers, transforming themselves into the apostles of

Christ. And no marvel; for Satan himself is transformed into an angel of light.

False apostles are emphasized in verse 13. They transform themselves into apostles of Christ. These verses indicate the setup of a false religious system.

Verse 4 of this same chapter tells that the false apostles will preach another Jesus, another gospel, and another spirit. In other words, they will pervert the true Gospel of Christ and will twist it to meet their own selfish needs and desires. They will appear to be from God:

2 Timothy 3:5

Having a form of godliness, but denying the power thereof ...

They will reason away and deny the supernatural power of God and will teach against everything supernatural. It is imperative for us to realize that without the power of God, we are no threat at all to Satan and his kingdom. Jesus said:

Mark 7:13

Making the word of God of none effect through

your tradition, which ye have delivered: and many such things do ye.

False apostles will set up traditions of men, specifically to make the Word of God ineffective. The most dangerous thing in a Christian's life is to reason along the lines of, "I believe" or "my church teaches." We must be open to the Word of God. If what you believe does not line up with His Word, you need to check what set of apostles you got it from.

When an apostle of God lays a foundation, he will use the Word of God. A false apostle will not be able to provide any strong biblical basis. He may have a verse or two, but it will be taken out of context. He will say things like, "Well, this is what has been taught for years now" or "we believe the Bible, but we also have our books of traditions." In this way, they make the Word of God of no effect in their lives. Thank God that we are not ignorant of Satan's devices:

2 Corinthians 2:11

Lest Satan should get an advantage of us: for we are not ignorant of his devices.

It is imperative that we know of the work of Satan's false apostles, that we know their methods and their teachings, so that the evil one does not gain an advantage over us.

I challenge you to look at what you teach in the light of what the fivefold ministry of God is saying. If the most part of the fivefold ministry of God disagrees with what you believe, if those who are standing in the power of God disagree with you, maybe you need to check your heart and search the Scriptures a little deeper to see why.

Chapter 7

The Prophet

Ephesians 2:19-22

> *Now therefore ye are no more strangers and foreigners, but fellowcitizens with the saints, and all of the household of God; and are built upon the foundation of the apostles and prophets, Jesus Christ himself being the chief corner stone; in whom all the building fitly framed together growth unto a holy temple in the Lord; in whom ye also are built together for an habitation of God through the Spirit.*

We have already seen that the prophet, along with the apostle, lays a foundation for the church. We know that the apostle lays a foundation in the Word or doctrine. Let's explore more deeply what the prophet does.

THE PROPHET OF GOD

1 Samuel 9:9

(Beforetime in Israel, when a man went to inquire of God, thus he spoke, Come, and let us go to the seer: for he that is now called a Prophet was beforetime called a Seer.)

He who is now called a prophet was once called a "seer." It is the prophet's job to see into the Spirit realm and tell us in the physical realm what he sees. If a man does not "see" in the Spirit realm, he is not a prophet. The gift of prophecy, as listed in 1 Corinthians 12, can be used by any Spirit-filled Christian:

1 Corinthians 12:7-11

But the manifestation of the Spirit is given to every man to profit withal. For to one is given by the Spirit the word of wisdom; to another the word of knowledge by the same Spirit; to another faith by the same Spirit; to another the gifts of healing by the same Spirit; to another the working of miracles; to another prophecy; to another discerning of spirits; to another divers kinds of tongues; to another the interpretation of tongues:

but all these worketh that one and the selfsame Spirit, dividing to every man severally as he will.

The simple gift of prophecy is for edification, exhortation, and comfort, as Paul taught:

1 Corinthians 14:3

But he that prophesieth speaketh unto men to edification, and exhortation, and comfort.

There is no revelation knowledge involved with this gift. What is spoken is only a good word to edify or comfort others. It lets you know that God is hearing you or moving on your behalf. It is equal to, or on the same level as, a message in tongues with the interpretation. Again, Paul taught:

1 Corinthians 14:5

I would that ye all spake with tongues but rather that ye prophesied: for greater is he that prophesieth than he that speaketh with tongues, except he interpret, that the church may receive edifying.

In this chapter, I am not addressing the gift of prophecy, but, rather, the "office" of a prophet.

To be a prophet, a saint must have at least one of the three revelation gifts working consistently in their life:

- Word of wisdom
- Word of knowledge
- Discerning of spirits

Again, Paul wrote:

1 Corinthians 12:8-10

For to one is given by the Spirit the word of wisdom; to another the word of knowledge by the same Spirit; to another faith by the same Spirit; to another the gifts of healing by the same Spirit; to another the working of miracles; to another prophecy; to another discerning of spirits; to another divers kinds of tongues; to another the interpretation of tongues.

THE PROPHETS OF GOD IN ACTION

I want to bring you to the New Testament and explore how prophets operate. We will examine how they tell what is happening in the supernatural realm:

The Prophet

Acts 11:27-30

> *And in these days came prophets from Jerusalem unto Antioch. And there stood up one of them named Agabus, and signified by the Spirit that there should be great dearth throughout all the world: which came to pass in the days of Claudius Caesar. Then the disciples, every man according to his ability, determined to send relief unto the brethren which dwelt in Judaea: which also they did, and sent it to the elders by the hands of Barnabas and Saul.*

Agabus, a prophet from Jerusalem, saw in the Spirit realm that a famine was about to come upon the world. Because of his warning, the church prepared and was not caught by surprise. One job of the prophet is to warn of things coming upon the earth. He is to warn of physical things that will happen. There are many examples of this in the Old Testament: Jeremiah, Joshua, Daniel, etc.

In the New Testament, the prophet is still preparing the Body of Christ for things to come. If we are listening to the prophets of God, we will not be caught by surprise. We are not to be subject to the elements of this world. If we listen to the prophets of God, we will be prepared for any crisis that comes.

Here's another example of prophets in the new Testament:

Acts 13:1-3

> *Now there were in the church that was at Antioch certain prophets and teachers; as Barnabas, and Simeon that was called Niger, and Lucius of Cyrene, and Manaen, which had been brought up with Herod, the tetrarch, and Saul. As they ministered to the Lord, and fasted, the Holy Ghost said, Separate me Barnabas and Saul for the work whereunto I have called them. And when they had fasted and prayed, and laid their hands on them, they sent them away.*

One point I want to be clear on is this: I agree that the Holy Ghost can speak in an audible voice (if He chooses to), but it does say there were prophets there to speak on God's behalf. As a general rule, we see the Spirit speaking through people. It is probably safe to say that the prophets spoke the clear word of direction, to separate Paul and Barnabas for their missionary calling.

Here we see the second job of a prophet, to give spiritual instructions to the Body. These instructions will bear witness with your spirit. Personal words need to be tested by the Word of God and also by your spirit. Do no struggle with them. If they are of God, they will come to pass. If not, let them go.

It would not be wise to test and judge the first job of a prophet, which is warning the church of things to come upon the earth. When a prophet warns of things to come, you'd better take heed, whether it bears witness with your spirit or not. When Jeremiah prophesied the Babylonian captivity, it did not bear witness with the other prophets. Regardless of whether or not they believed, it came to pass.

We must listen to the prophets. A prophet named Agabus prophesied something very unusual in New Testament times:

Acts 21:10-11

And as we tarried there many days, there came down from Judea a certain prophet, named Agabus. And when he was come unto us, he took Paul's girdle, and bound his own hands and feet, and said, Thus saith the Holy Ghost, So shall the Jews at Jerusalem bind the man that owneth this girdle, and shall deliver him into the hands of the Gentiles.

121

Agabus warned the apostle Paul of the trials and attacks of Satan to come upon him. The saint of God is not subject to whatever Satan wants to do. If we submit to the office of a prophet, we will know the acts of the enemy before he does them. This prepares us to be ready to fight instead of being caught off guard.

In my own life, listening to the prophets has made the good fight of faith much easier. When you know the enemy's plan, he is defeated before he gets started.

THE FALSE PROPHETS

What about the false prophet? Once again, let us take a look at Ephesians 6:

Ephesians 6:11-12

Put on the whole armour of God, that ye may be able to stand against the wiles of the devil. For we wrestle not against flesh and blood, but against principalities, against powers, against the rulers of the darkness of this world, against spiritual wickedness in high places.

Remember, we said that the second level would have to fight against the prophet and aid the false prophets. The second thing listed here is *principalities*. Let's see if they fight against the prophets of God.

DANIEL WAS HINDERED BY THE PRINCE OF PERSIA

Daniel 10:11-14

And he said unto me, O Daniel, a man greatly beloved, understand the words that I speak unto thee, and stand upright: for unto thee am I now sent. And when he had spoken this word unto me, I stood trembling.

Then said he unto me, Fear not, Daniel: for from the first day that thou didst set thine heart to understand, and to chasten thyself before thy God, thy words were heard, and I am come for thy words. But the prince of the kingdom of Persia withstood me one and twenty days: but, lo, Michael, one of the chief princes, came to help me; and I remained there with the kings of Persia. Now I am come to make thee understand what shall befall thy people in the latter days: for yet the vision is for many days.

In this passage, the prince of Persia was standing to fight against and stop the prophet Daniel from receiving a word from God. Note that the spiritual entity, or demon, over Persia, identified as the Prince of Persia himself, was fighting to stop Daniel the prophet from seeing into or receiving information from the Spirit realm.

Paul Fought a False Prophet

Let's look at another example of a false prophet found in the book of Acts:

Acts 13:6-11

And when they had gone through the isle unto Pathos, they found a certain sorcerer, a false prophet, a Jew, whose name was Barjesus: which was with the deputy of the country, Sergius Paulus, a prudent man; who called for Barnabas and Saul, and desired to hear the word of God. But Elymas the sorcerer (for so is his name by interpretation) withstood them, seeking to turn away the deputy from the faith. Then Saul, (who also is called Paul,) filled with the Holy Ghost, set his eyes on him. And said, O full of all subtilty and all mischief, thou child of the devil, thou enemy of all righteousness, wilt thou not cease to pervert the right ways of the Lord? And now, behold, the hand of the Lord is upon thee, and thou shalt be blind, not seeing the sun for a season. And immediately there fell on him a mist and a darkness; and he went about seeking some to lead him by the hand.

Paul, as an apostle and prophet, was having a battle with a false prophet. For a clear understanding, I want to identify the office of a false prophet. Note that, through sorcery or seeing into the spirit realm by devils, this sorcerer led the deputy of the country. False prophets will seek to influence powerful men in the world so that they, in turn, may influence others through them.

False prophets will lead men in things to come, just as the Holy Ghost, working through the prophet of God, leads us. However the false prophet does so by being led by the "principality" over that particular area in the spirit realm.

The Scriptures are very clear on the things we are to stay away from:

Deuteronomy 18:10-14

There shall not be found among you any one that maketh his son or his daughter to pass through the fire, or that useth divination, or an observer of times, or an enchanter, or a witch. Or a charmer, or a consulter with familiar spirits, or a wizard, or a necromancer. For all that do these things are an abomination unto the LORD: and because of these abominations the LORD thy God doth drive them out from before thee. Thou shalt be perfect with the LORD thy God.

For these nations, which thou shalt possess, hearkened unto observers of times, and unto diviners: but as for thee, the LORD thy God hath not suffered thee so to do.

I want to be as clear as I can: It is not okay to get your palm read. It is not okay to obtain any information by means of tarot cards or horoscopes, etc. These are abominations unto the Lord. Never before has there been so much of this type of activity in our nation. Television and the Internet provide easy access to listen to and get in touch with witches. But this is sin!

Verse 15 of this passage is of critical importance:

Deuteronomy 18:15

The LORD thy God will raise up unto thee a Prophet from the midst of thee, of thy brethren, like unto me; unto him ye shall hearken.

"Unto him ye shall hearken." You are to call on the prophet of God, for God will raise up one like you, to be His prophet. If you need to know something in the Spirit realm, you are instructed by the Word of God to call on the prophets:

2 Chronicles 20:20

> *And they rose early in the morning, and went forth into the wilderness of Tekoa: and as they went forth, Jehoshaphat stood and said, Hear me, O Judah, and ye inhabitants of Jerusalem; Believe in the LORD your God, so shall ye be established; believe his prophets, so shall ye prosper.*

Believe in and rely on the prophet of God, and you will not be caught by surprise in the physical things of this life or the spiritual things of your Christian walk. Then, and only then, will you prosper.

Chapter 8

The Evangelist

Acts 21:8-9

> *And the next day we that were of Paul's com-*
> *pany departed, and came unto Caesarea: and we*
> *entered into the house of Philip the evangelist,*
> *which was one of the seven; and abode with him.*
> *And the same man had four daughters, virgins,*
> *which did prophesy.*

THE EVANGELIST OF GOD IN ACTION

Philip was an evangelist for God. Notice that his household was one of godliness. Even his daughters prophesied. Let's take a closer look at Philip, to learn more about the evangelist:

Acts 8:5-8

> *Then Philip went down to the city of Samaria, and preached Christ unto them. And the people with one accord gave heed unto those things which Philip spake, hearing and seeing the miracles which he did. For unclean spirits, crying with loud voice, came out of many that were possessed with them: and many taken with palsies, and that were lame, were healed. And there was great joy in that city.*

Philip exercised the three power gifts of the Holy Spirit—faith, miracles, and healings. First Corinthians 12 identifies the power gifts from the Holy Spirit and shows how the evangelist flows and works in the Body of Christ.

FAITH

1 John 5:4

> *For whatsoever is born of God overcometh the world: and this is the victory that overcometh the world, even our faith.*

The evangelist will move in a faith that overcomes the world. He will have the faith to believe for you, no matter what your problem or need. When no one else has the answer, the evangelist will have the faith to change things. Men like R.W. Schambach and Billy Graham were perfect examples of evangelists with faith that overcame the world.

MIRACLES

John 2:11

> *This beginning of miracles did Jesus in Cana of Galilee, and manifested forth his glory; and his disciples believed on him.*

Miracles are always for people to believe on Jesus, not the evangelist. If the evangelist takes the glory, the signs are not from God. Mark tells us that signs come to confirm God's Word:

Mark 16:20

> *And they went forth, and preached every where, the Lord working with them, and confirming the word with signs following. Amen.*

The evangelist will do many signs. God will bring finances, fix marriages, and provide answers to the worst situations through the evangelist, to confirm the Word that he is bringing to the church.

HEALINGS

Because of the faith and miracles being manifested through the evangelist, the faith of the congregation will be at a high level for healing. Let's focus our attention again on what happened in Acts 8:

Acts 8:8

and there was great joy in the city.

Take particular notice that the office of evangelist brings great joy into a city, not just to the Body of Christ or church congregation. It is the job of the evangelist to stir up the people, not to establish the church.

We see, in Acts 8:14-17, that the apostles came to Samaria from Jerusalem to establish the church:

Acts 8:14-17

Now when the apostles which were at Jerusalem heard that Samaria had received

131

the word of God, they sent unto them Peter and John: who, when they were come down, prayed for them, that they might receive the Holy Ghost: (for as yet he was fallen upon none of them: only they were baptized in the name of the Lord Jesus.) Then laid they their hands on them, and they received the Holy Ghost.

As soon as the church was established, the evangelist departed:

Acts 8:26

And the angel of the Lord spake unto Philip, saying, Arise, and go toward the south unto the way that goeth down from Jerusalem unto Gaza, which is desert.

I want to make it clear: the evangelist does not feed the flock or watch over them. We will learn in the next chapter that the pastor does this. Never be guilty of saying, "If my pastor only moved in the Spirit like the evangelist, the church would grow." It's not the pastor's job to do that. He is the pastor.

THE FALSE EVANGELIST

What about the false evangelist? Looking back at Ephesians 6:11-12 again, we see that *powers* is listed as the third element in what the Holy Spirit identified as the fivefold ministry of Satan. Let's see if the *powers* fight against the evangelist and, if so, how:

Acts 8:9-11

> *But there was a certain man, called Simon, which beforetime in the same city used sorcery, and bewitched the people of Samaria, giving out that himself was some great one: to whom they all gave heed, from the least to the greatest, saying, This man is the great power of God. And to him they had regard, because that of long time he had bewitched them with sorceries.*

Simon had bewitched the people of Samaria and had the whole city thinking that he was *"the great power of God."* He did the same things Philip did, except that he used witchcraft to do them. It is evident that Simon, using the powers of darkness, had successfully counterfeited the role of the evangelist by stirring up the city.

Take note that Simon himself gave out that he was *"some great one."* This will always be the case, when there are false signs and wonders:

2 Thessalonians 2:9-11

> *Even him, whose coming is after the work-*
> *ing of Satan with all power and signs and*
> *lying wonders, and with all deceivableness of*
> *unrighteousness in them that perish; because*
> *they received not the love of the truth, that they*
> *might be saved. And for this cause God shall*
> *send them strong delusion, that they should*
> *believe a lie.*

In verse 9, a counterfeit of the gifts is being set up. Verses 10 and 11 make it clear that because they received not the love of the truth, these false powers were able to be established. If you don't have a love for God's Word, if you don't have a love for and submission to His authoritative structure, you are in great danger of being deceived:

Acts 17:11

> *These were more noble than those in*
> *Thessalonica, in that they received the word*

with all readiness of mind, and searched the
scriptures daily, whether those things were so.

One reason these people were considered *"noble"* was that they received the Word *"with all readiness of mind."* They wanted to hear everything Paul and Silas had to say to them, not just what they wanted to hear. They were hungry for what the Word said.

Second, after listening to all that Paul and Silas had to say, they searched the Scriptures daily to see if it was so. Paul wrote to Timothy:

2 Timothy 2:15

Study to show thyself approved unto God,
a workman that needeth not to be ashamed,
rightly dividing the word of truth.

If you study the Word as *"unto God,"* you will not be ashamed or deceived. This is a promise from God Himself!

Chapter 9

The Pastor

Titus 1:4-5

> *To Titus, mine own son after the common faith:*
> *Grace, mercy, and peace, from God the Father*
> *and the Lord Jesus Christ our Saviour. For this*
> *cause left I thee in Crete, that thou shouldest set*
> *in order the things that are wanting, and ordain*
> *elders in every city, as I had appointed thee.*

GOD'S PASTOR IN ACTION

Here was a young pastor, Titus, left in Crete by the apostle Paul. His job was to set in order the work that the apostle had established. Here we can begin to see how the five ministry gifts work hand in hand with each other.

Titus, in the role of pastor, was to set the church in order and ordain elders as the apostle (Paul) had appointed. The apostle had already laid the foundation for what the pastor, in this case, Titus, was to teach. Paul, the apostle, went on in the next four verses to lay the foundation, or outline, for what the pastor's job is. He is to govern over the individual body and raise up the next line of the fivefold ministry.

In God, there is no great or small. Every part of the Body of Christ is just as important as the rest:

1 Corinthians 12:14-27

For the body is not one member, but many. If the foot shall say, Because I am not the hand, I am not of the body; is it therefore not of the body? And if the ear shall say, Because I am not the eye, I am not of the body; is it therefore not of the body? If the whole body were an eye, where were the hearing? If the whole were hearing, where were the smelling? But now hath God set the members every one of them in the body, as it hath pleased him. And if they were all one member, where were the body? But now are they many members, yet but one body.

And the eye cannot say unto the hand, I have no need of thee: nor again the head to the feet, I have no need of you. Nay, much more those members of the body, which seem to be more feeble, are necessary: and those members of the body, which we think to be less honourable, upon these we bestow more abundant honour; and our uncomely parts have more abundant comeliness. For our comely parts have no need: but God hath tempered the body together, having given more abundant honour to that part which lacked. That there should be no schism in the body; but that the members should have the same care one for another. And whether one member suffer, all the members suffer with it; or one member be honoured, all the members rejoice with it. Now ye are the body of Christ, and members in particular.

In fact, Jesus said, *"whosoever of you will be the chiefest, shall be servant of all"* (Mark 10:44).

The pastor must speak *"sound doctrine"*:

Titus 2:1

But speak thou the things which become sound doctrine.

The pastor must be very careful. Whatever the pastor does, the body that he governs over will also do. Whatever he says, they will also say. The part of the body he governs will not receive or flow in areas he disapproves of. Paul wrote to Timothy:

1 Timothy 4:6-16

If thou put the brethren in remembrance of these things, thou shalt be a good minister of Jesus Christ, nourished up in the words of faith and of good doctrine, whereunto thou hast attained. But refuse profane and old wives' fables, and exercise thyself rather unto godliness. For bodily exercise profiteth little: but godliness is profitable unto all things, having promise of the life that now is, and of that which is to come. This is a faithful saying and worthy of all acceptation. For therefore we both labour and suffer reproach, because we trust in the living God, who is the Saviour of all men, specially of those that believe.

These things command and teach. Let no man despise thy youth; but be thou an example of the believers, in word, in conversation, in charity, in spirit, in faith, in purity. Till I come, give attendance to reading, to exhortation, to doctrine. Neglect not the gift that is in thee, which was given thee by prophecy, with the laying on of the hands of the presbytery.

Meditate upon these things; give thyself wholly to them; that thy profiting may appear to all. Take heed unto thyself, and unto the doctrine; continue in them: for in doing this thou shalt both save thyself, and them that hear thee.

Timothy was another young pastor whom the apostle Paul had left in Ephesus:

1 Timothy 1:2-4

Unto Timothy, my own son in the faith: Grace, mercy, and peace, from God our Father and Jesus Christ our Lord. As I besought thee to abide still at Ephesus, when I went into Macedonia, that thou mightest charge some that they teach no other doctrine, neither give heed to fables and endless genealogies, which minister questions, rather than godly edifying which is in faith: so do.

Timothy was commissioned to remind the brethren of good doctrine and to put an end to all the *"fables"* and *"endless genealogies."* It is the pastor's job to get all the old "I believe that's" out of the Body of Christ. They are to feed their people pure doctrine, which provides godly edification for the Body.

The pastor is to be an example to the believers. His main responsibility is the church. It is not his job to bring great joy to the city. That's the job of the evangelist. However, we should also note here, Timothy was told to also *"do the work of an evangelist"*:

2 Timothy 4:4-5

And they shall turn away their ears from the truth, and shall be turned unto fables. But watch thou in all things, endure afflictions, do the work of an evangelist, make full proof of thy ministry.

Paul, as an apostle, filled the office of a teacher and pastor at times. The pastor should have a vision for the city, but his main responsibility is to feed the Body. As we have seen, Paul wrote:

1 Timothy 4:13-16

Till I come, give attendance to reading, to exhortation, to doctrine. Neglect not the gift that is in thee, which was given thee by prophecy, with the laying on of the hands of the presbytery. Meditate upon these things; give thyself wholly to them; that thy profiting may appear to all. Take heed unto thyself, and unto the doctrine; continue in them: for in doing this thou shalt both save thyself and them that hear thee.

The apostle (Paul) admonished the pastor (Timothy) to take heed unto himself and the doctrine. He told him *"continue in them."* In doing so, he assured him, he would both save himself and those who heard him. This serves to emphasize that whatever the pastor does not only affects him, but also the whole body he governs:

Hebrews 13:17

Obey them that have the rule over you, and submit yourselves: for they watch for your souls, as they that must give account, that they may do it with joy, and not with grief: for that is unprofitable for you.

The church probably has more problems with this than anything else in the Bible. If you cannot obey your pastor, if you cannot submit to what he says the church needs, that's a problem between you and God. The problem is not just between you and your pastor.

God puts pastors in office and gives them unique wisdom and insight that He gives no one else, for governing the church. Not even the prophet can override the pastoral office. This is interesting because the prophet has special insight and can see all things:

Amos 3:7

> *Surely the LORD God will do nothing, but he revealeth his secret unto his servants the prophets.*

The pastor sees the need and direction of that individual body, because God is moving in him. This has nothing to do with him personally, as an individual. It has everything to do with the fivefold ministry office of the pastor. If you find yourself in disagreement with your pastor, or you think he is wrong, submit to him anyway. God will lead him, as you pray for him. You may find yourself promoted for your obedience and submission.

I remember an occasion in which I and my pastor, a powerful man of God, disagreed. I had four pages of notes, mostly scripture references, on why I was right, and he gave me just one verse on why he was right. Through the grace of God, I was able to submit to him as my pastor anyway.

He had requested me not to use a certain supernatural gift. Needless to say, I prayed very intently about the matter, but I obeyed his request. Since then, I have seen him flowing in the thing he didn't understand, didn't accept, and, at first, didn't allow. After that incident, God promoted me greatly in that church. Oh, it never ceases to amaze me what God will do when we begin to flow as a body instead of fighting each other!

Truly, if we, as God's sheep, would totally submit ourselves to His fivefold ministry, we would become that perfect man in Christ Jesus.

THE FALSE PASTOR IN ACTION

Let's examine the next office in Ephesians 6:11-12. The fourth office the Holy Spirit showed me was the *rulers of the darkness of this world*. This position, the counterfeit pastor, fights against

144

pastors. We can see by their title, *"rulers of the darkness of this world,"* that they are the elements of Satan's spiritual hierarchy that govern over his kingdom and their followers, the false body, just as God's pastors govern over their portion of the Body of Christ:

2 Corinthians 11:13-15

> *For such are false apostles, deceitful workers, transforming themselves into the apostles of Christ. And no marvel; for Satan himself is transformed into an angel of light. Therefore it is no great thing if his ministers also be transformed as the ministers of righteousness; whose end shall be according to their works.*

False ministers (or pastors) are transformed into minsters of light. They will govern the bodies that the false apostles establish, laying down a false word. Remember, we said the false apostles would set up a religious system founded on the traditions of men, to make the Word of God ineffective.

Just as the apostle Paul had Timothy and Titus pastoring over the churches he established in the Lord, so does the false apostle have rulers

145

of darkness over their respective areas, as minsters of Satan:

Titus 1:9-13

Holding fast the faithful word as he hath been taught, that he may be able by sound doctrine both to exhort and to convince the gainsayers. For there are many unruly and vain talkers and deceivers, specially they of the circumcision: whose mouths must be stopped, who subvert whole houses, teaching things which they ought not, for filthy lucre's sake. One of themselves, even a prophet of their own, said, the Cretians are always liars, evil beasts, slow bellies. This witness is true. Wherefore rebuke them sharply, that they may be sound in the faith.

Here, Paul (the apostle) was instructing the pastor (Titus) to stop the false pastors who were unruly, vain talkers, and deceivers, from teaching things they ought not to teach. They were doing it for the sake of money. Paul exhorted Timothy:

2 Timothy 2:16-18

But shun profane and vain babblings: for they will increase unto more ungodliness. And their word will eat as doth a canker: of whom is Hymenaeus and Philetus; who concerning the truth have erred, saying that the resurrection is past already; and overthrow the faith of some.

Note that Timothy was told to shun, or put an end to, the false pastors who taught vain babblings and things that were not true.

Peter exhorted:

1 Peter 5:1-4

The elders which are among you I exhort, who am also an elder, and a witness of the sufferings of Christ, and also a partaker of the glory that shall be revealed: Feed the flock of God which is among you, taking the oversight thereof, not by constraint, but willingly; not for filthy lucre, but of a ready mind; neither as being lords over God's heritage, but being examples to the flock. And when the chief Shepherd shall appear, ye shall receive a crown of glory that fadeth not away.

This passage of scripture lists several characteristics of a pastor as he attends to his flock and contrasts them with false pastors. The true pastor will lead, but he will lead by example. The false pastor will lead by constraint. The true pastor will lead by love, but the false pastor will lead by fear.

In my years of pastoring, I have observed a very deep hunger from the congregation for the unadulterated Word of God. My constant prayer is that God would send us more pastors who lead by love and example, pastors who are dedicated and faithful to their call.

Chapter 10

The Teacher

Galatians 6:6

Let him that is taught in the word communicate unto him that teacheth in all good things.

THE TEACHER OF GOD

It is the teacher's job to communicate with the people in all their personal circumstances. He helps the pastor to disciple his flock. The pastor cannot possibly disciple all the people in the body. Therefore, we have the teachers (Sunday school teachers, Children's Church teachers, Boy's Camp teachers, etc.). Teachers are always to submit to and follow the vision of the pastor. The teacher should raise up and disciple people to work with the pastor. The teacher will teach others what he hears from the pastor. He will be the one who is there to encourage you when you are undergoing bad times. Grounded in the Word, he will help to ground others in the Word.

In Acts 11, we see the astonishing results of good teaching:

Acts 11:25-26

> *Then departed Barnabas to Tarsus, for to seek Saul: and when he had found him, he brought him unto Antioch. And it came to pass, that a whole year they assembled themselves with the church, and taught much people. And the disciples were called Christians first in Antioch.*

Paul and Barnabas were working in the office of a teacher, and the stunning result was that people were called Christians for the first time. The teacher's major responsibility is to work with the church, the body of believers, on an individual basis, to conform them to the image of Christ.

The teacher is probably the most abused person in the Body. They are never in the limelight. Often, we forget to tell them how important they are to the Body of Christ. We send our children to their classes, while we sit in the main service and enjoy the spiritual food the pastor is setting forth. The teacher is in the back, serving and not being served. Personally, I take my hat off to the many teachers who get little or no recognition—and don't ask for any.

In a situation like this, I get a little more insight into what Jesus meant when He said that those who have a desire to be first shall be *"last of all"* and *"servant of all"*:

Mark 9:34-35

> *But they held their peace: for by the way they had disputed among themselves, who should be the greatest. And he sat down, and called the twelve, and saith unto them, If any man desire to be first, the same shall be last of all, and servant of all.*

It is especially good to notice that Jesus said this to His disciples after they had been arguing among themselves about who should be the greatest. I do not know a mature teacher who displays this attitude. The teacher, as a servant to the Body of Christ, may be the greatest of the

151

entire fivefold ministry. Didn't Jesus say the last would be first and the first last?

Matthew 20:16

So the last shall be first, and the first last: for many be called, but few chosen.

The False Teacher in Action

What about the false teacher? Once again, let us look at Ephesians 6:11-12. The last office the Holy Spirit told me about in Satan's fivefold ministry is *"spiritual wickedness in high places."* These are wicked spirits that go out to teach or lead believers away from the image of Christ:

1 Timothy 4:1-2

Now the Spirit speaketh expressly, that in the latter times some shall depart from the faith, giving heed to seducing spirits, and doctrines of devils; speaking lies in hypocrisy; having their conscience seared with a hot iron.

2 Timothy 4:3-4

For the time will come when they will not endure sound doctrine; but after their own lusts shall they heap to themselves teachers, having itching ears; and they shall turn away their ears from the truth, and shall be turned unto fables.

HOW TO IDENTIFY THE FALSE TEACHER

The false teacher will emerge and flourish in the condition mentioned in 2 Timothy 4:3: *"They will not endure sound doctrine ... , but ... heap to themselves teachers."* The false teacher will do just the opposite of the teacher of God. The false teacher will put forth lies, fables, and seducing words that tickle the ears of the people. Their doctrine will minister to the flesh. They will teach things that cause men and women to conform to the world or the flesh, not to the image of Christ.

The false teacher will not be submitted to a pastor, for he will think he knows more than the pastor. He will say things like, "You don't need to be under a pastor," or "Church is where two or more gather together," to justify his rebellious attitude.

MY DEEP-FELT ADVICE

If this is your attitude, I urge you, brethren: Listen to me and to God! You are in dangerous territory. I would urge anyone who has this mindset to heed (and I strongly emphasize HEED) what God says in the book of Hebrews:

Hebrews 10:25

> *Not forsaking the assembling of ourselves together, as the manner of some is; but exhorting one another: and so much the more, as ye see the day approaching.*

This is a very clear spiritual admonition and warning. What does it mean? It means exactly what is says. We must not forsake the assembling of ourselves together.

John wrote to the churches of his day:

1 John 1:7

> *But if we walk in the light, as he is in the light, we have fellowship one with another, and the blood of Jesus Christ his Son cleanseth us from all sin.*

Our victory comes from walking in the light and continuing to have fellowship with God's people. Whatever you do, don't let false teachers draw you away on your own. If someone's teachings minister to your flesh and your spirit is grieved, he is probably a false teacher. If what he says leads you away from the Body of Christ, it is not the Holy Spirit. The Holy Spirit will always lead you to the Body of Christ and the authoritative structure of the fivefold ministry of God.

In Conclusion

This revelation of the five-fold ministry that God downloaded into my spirit has moved me into a deeper, more excellent walk with Him, and the scriptures I have gone over throughout these chapters have created an amazing dynamic to the foundation I walk in today. I trust they will do the same for you.

Part III

Life in the Garden

Chapter 11

Living in the Glory of God's Presence

The third revelation, the one that makes up this last portion of the book, was of a beautiful garden, the garden of God. As I beheld it, I realized that God has so much more for us than we have thus far realized. His will is that we walk in His presence, hear His voice and experience His glory, not just once in a great while, but every moment of every day.

The garden was so beautiful, and it was created for you and me. It was created for our enjoyment, for our provision, and for our advancement. It is the place where we can experience the most peace, perfect peace, and the place where we can feel totally secure in who we are in Christ. Living in this place will bring us to our highest potential, both in our physical life, and in our walk in the Kingdom of God. There's no place that can compare with the garden of God.

It all began for me one Wednesday night during our regular worship service. I was feeling the presence of God, worshiping Jesus for who He is, and suddenly I was somewhere else, somewhere very different, very wonderful. God was giving me a very personal peek into His garden.

As I neared the entrance, I realized where I was. One of the first things I saw were the cherubims and the flaming sword turning in all directions, guarding the way into that holy place. As glorious as these were, I could hardly wait to get past them and get a taste of the Tree of Life and drink from the river of living water. It was every bit as wonderful as I had imagined!

When the vision eventually lifted, one of the prophets in our church began proclaiming a word from the Lord. He said: "The Lord is calling us to the garden where everything began and everything will end." This prophet had no idea what I had just experienced. This sent me on a journey to understand what I had seen. I needed to know why everything began in that garden and why everything would end there.

What was in the garden that made it so valuable? Are the things there available to me now? If so, how do I get them? And how do I get into the garden, past the cherubims and the flaming sword?

My search began in the book of beginnings:

Genesis 3:22-24

And the LORD God said, Behold, the man is become as one of us, to know good and evil: and now, lest he put forth his hand, and take also of the tree of life, and eat, and live for ever: therefore the LORD God sent him forth from the garden of Eden, to till the ground from whence he was taken. So he drove out the man; and he placed at the east of the garden of Eden Cherubims, and a flaming sword which turned every way, to keep the way of the tree of life.

Sadly, the garden of God is now a place forbidden to man. Those cherubims and that flaming sword are there to keep him out.

As for the cherubims themselves, here is the best picture we have of them in the Scriptures:

Ezekiel 10:1-16

Then I looked, and, behold, in the firmament that was above the head of the cherubims there appeared over them as it were a sapphire stone, as the appearance of the likeness of a throne. And he spake unto the man clothed with linen, and said, Go in between the wheels, even under the cherub, and fill thine hand with coals of fire from between the cherubims, and scatter them over the city. And he went in in my sight. Now the cherubims stood on the right side of the house, when the man went in; and the cloud filled the inner court. Then the glory of the LORD went up from the cherub, and stood over the threshold of the house; and the house was filled with the cloud, and the court was full of the brightness of the LORD's glory. And the sound of the cherubims' wings was heard even to the outer court, as the voice of the Almighty God when he speaketh.

And it came to pass, that when he had commanded the man clothed with linen, saying, Take fire from between the wheels, from between the cherubims; then he went in, and stood beside the wheels. And one cherub stretched forth his hand from between the cherubims unto the fire that was between the cherubims, and took thereof, and put it into the hands of him that was clothed with linen: who took it, and went out. And there appeared in the cherubims the form of a man's hand under their wings.

And when I looked, behold the four wheels by the cherubims, one wheel by one cherub, and another wheel by another cherub: and the appearance of the wheels was as the colour of a beryl stone. And as for their appearances, they four had one likeness, as if a wheel had been in the midst of a wheel. When they went, they went upon their four sides; they turned not as they went, but to the place whither the head looked they followed it; they turned not as they went. And their whole body, and their backs, and their hands, and their wings, and the wheels, were full of eyes round about, even the wheels that they four had. As for the wheels, it was cried unto them in my hearing, O wheel. And every one had four faces: the first face was the face of a cherub, and the second face was the face of a man, and the third the face of a lion, and the fourth the face of an eagle.

And the cherubims were lifted up. This is the living creature that I saw by the river of

Chebar. And when the cherubims went, the wheels went by them: and when the cherubims lifted up their wings to mount up from the earth, the same wheels also turned not from beside them.

That should be enough to stop anyone in their tracks. But to add to that this fact: there in the garden is a sword on fire and moving by itself, as if it were alive. It would seem that there is little to no hope of us getting past these and going in there.

THE INVITATION

But wait! The Bible has more to say about us entering into the garden. Let's look further:

Revelation 22:12-17

And, behold, I come quickly; and my reward is with me, to give every man according as his work shall be. I am Alpha and Omega, the beginning and the end, the first and the last. Blessed are they that do his commandments, that they may have right to the tree of life, and may enter in through the gates into the city. For without are dogs, and sorcerers, and whoremongers, and murderers, and idolaters, and whosoever loveth and maketh a lie.

I Jesus have sent mine angel to testify unto you these things in the churches. I am the root and the offspring of David, and the bright and morning star.

And the Spirit and the bride say, Come. And let him that heareth say, Come. And let him that is athirst come. And whosoever will, let him take the water of life freely.

So, if I obey God's commandments, I have a right (a right given to me by Jesus Himself) to partake of the Tree of Life. I can enter in through the gates into God's garden.

Jesus has made special gates just for you and me and all those who belong to Him and obey His Word. Not only do you have the right, but the Spirit and the Bride are giving you an open invitation to drink from the water of life. Both the tree and the water are in the garden of God.

Do you need more? Okay!

Revelation 2:7

He that hath an ear, let him hear what the Spirit saith unto the churches; To him that overcometh will I give to eat of the tree of life, which is in the midst of the paradise of God.

Overcomers are given the right to eat from the Tree of Life, which is in the midst of God's garden. So, the only things keeping us out of the garden would be things we need to deal with, as the Spirit prompts. We must allow Him to remove them from our lives so that we can enter and enjoy God's bounty.

MY PEEK INTO THE GARDEN

My curiosity and excitement about the garden continued to grow in intensity. I wanted to know what was in that garden and how those things would apply to me. I discovered two descriptions of the garden, the first one in Genesis:

Genesis 2:8-10

And the LORD God planted a garden eastward in Eden; and there he put the man whom he had formed. And out of the ground made the LORD God to grow every tree that is pleasant to the sight, and good for food; the tree of life also in the midst of the garden, and the tree of knowledge of good and evil. And a river went out of Eden to water the garden; and from thence it was parted, and became into four heads.

It is clear that every tree good for food is to be found in God's garden. When I shared this with my wife, Vanessa, she got excited. She is a big garden hobbyist. She loves planting and growing things. Our home is surrounded with all kinds of fruit trees, as well as a garden filled with fresh vegetables. It is a wonderful experience to walk through the yard and pick things off the vine, eating them ripe and fresh!

There are also two other trees in the garden of God, one of them good and the other bad. One tree gives life, and the other tree gives death. So, in the garden, you still have the opportunity for obeying God or disobeying Him.

There is also a river in the garden that parts into four steams. These water the garden. Without water there is no life, right?

I found the second description of God's garden in Revelation:

Revelation 22:1-2

And he shewed me a pure river of water of life, clear as crystal, proceeding out of the throne of God and of the Lamb. In the midst of the street of it, and on either side of the river, was there the tree of life, which bare twelve manner of fruits, and yielded her fruit every month: and the leaves of the tree were for the healing of the nations.

According to the Scriptures, the river flows straight out of the throne of God and the Lamb Himself. So, the garden is tied to the throne of God by the river, and its life source, the river, flows from Jesus, the Living Water.

The Tree of Life bears twelve fruits, a different fruit each month. The leaves of the Tree of Life are for your healing.

As I continued to examine the depth of this scripture, the Lord revealed to me how the tree and the river would apply to my life in the here and now.

THE TREE

Again, let's read from Revelation:

Revelation 22:1-2

And he shewed me a pure river of water of life, clear as crystal, proceeding out of the throne of God and of the Lamb. In the midst of the street of it, and on either side of the river, was there the tree of life, which bare twelve manner of fruits, and yielded her fruit every month: and the leaves of the tree were for the healing of the nations.

There is a river flowing out of the throne of God and out of Jesus Himself, and, on either side of it there is the Tree of Life. Either there are two trees of life, or the river flows through the middle of the Tree of Life. Either way, the Tree of Life keeps the two banks of the River of Life on course.

As I noted, I live in South Louisiana and love to fish. One of my favorite bayous has trees growing on both sides of it. It is impossible to miss the path of the water. This is a big help to keep from running aground. That's because the trees on either side keep you in the bayou.

I have another wonderful fishing spot where the bayou has marsh on both sides. If the tide is up, you have to know where to navigate your boat, or you will find yourself stuck in the marsh. The marsh mud becomes like quicksand and bogs the boat down. Then, since the boat motor needs water to cool its engine, it quickly overheats and shuts down. What a disaster! Getting stuck in the marsh can be a long and difficult challenge that can ruin a good fishing trip.

This is the picture I get when thinking about the Tree of Life and the River of Life. Partaking of the tree and its fruits will keep you in the river, enjoying all it has to offer. It will also prevent you from getting stuck in the marsh.

As noted, the Tree of Life bears twelve different fruits. It produces a different fruit each month. When you eat from it, the month (or season of life) you're in, will determine the fruit it has for you.

The word for *fruit* in the original text is *karpos* and means "plucked." It comes from the root word *har-pad'-zo*, and it means "to seize or take away." So we can say the fruits of the Tree of Life are the takeaway we pluck from life's lessons.

Wisdom at every point of life is a takeaway that will keep you in the river. When we respond to wisdom and learn the lesson she has for us, we never end up stuck in the marsh. If you find yourself stuck, not going anywhere in life or with God, revisit the last thing God tried to teach you. God has more for you to learn and apply in that particular season of your life.

Then there are the leaves, which are for the healing of the nations. The original text used the word *fool'-lon*, which simply means "a sprout or leaf," but it comes from the root word *foo-lay'*, which means "offshoot, race, kindred, or tribe." God put me in a tribe, or race, for my healing, and the tribe He put you in has what you need to stay healthy.

We can even apply this to the part of the Body of Christ you belong to. Jesus put me into the Foursquare Gospel tribe of the Body of Christ. So, as I submit to the leadership of the Foursquare Church, it keeps me firmly in the River of Life. If I were to get out on my own, thinking I knew everything about God's plan, I might just find myself stuck in the marsh.

I don't have to agree with everything my tribe teaches, and I don't, but Jesus put me in this tribe. So, if I want to stay healthy and enjoy the river that runs through the tribe, I must stay in the tribe Jesus put me in.

That's not to say that God will not move you, as your season of life changes. But you'd better know it is Jesus, and not an offence, that is moving you.

THE HOW OF IT

Let us now look at how to get into the garden and eat from the Tree of Life. Jesus, in Revelation 2:4-7, gives us this instruction:

Revelation 2:4-7

Nevertheless I have somewhat against thee, because thou hast left thy first love. Remember therefore from whence thou art fallen, and repent, and do the first works; or else I will come unto thee quickly, and will remove thy candlestick out of his place, except thou repent. But this thou hast, that thou hatest the deeds of the Nicolaitans, which I also hate. He that hath an ear, let him hear what the Spirit saith unto the churches; To him that overcometh will I give to eat of the tree of life, which is in the midst of the paradise of God.

Here, Jesus tells us that if we will do three things, He will give us to eat from the Tree of Life. Remember the words *do* and *hate*.

First, remember from where you are fallen. Look back to the takeaways from life and repent. Learn what wisdom told you to do and not do. Let these life lessons be your guide.

Second, apply the fruits of each season to your life. If you are not applying the fruit, you'll get stuck in that season. You'll get out of the river and stuck in the marsh.

Third, hate the deeds of the Nicolaitans. Who were these people? And why did Jesus hate their deeds? And why would eating from the Tree of Life be allowed for hating those deeds?

The Nicolaitans, it is commonly thought, were a sect of Gnostics who taught the most impure doctrines and had the most impure practices. They are thought to have derived from Nicolas, one of the seven deacons mentioned in Acts 6:5.

Sadly, the Nicolaitans taught the community of wives that adultery and fornication were not serous sins. They also taught that eating meats offered to idols was quite lawful, and they mixed several pagan rites with Christian ceremonies.

According to *Adam Clarke's Commentary*,[1] everything that the Nicolaitans taught is opposite from the truths of the Tree of Life. Their main

1. **Adam Clarke and Ralph Earle, (Kansas City, MO: Beacon Hill Press of Kansas City, 1967)**

ideology was to compromise with pagan rites, to avoid persecution. This would be equivalent to getting out of your tribe and losing your right to the fruits of the Tree of Life.

THE TWO BANKS OF THE RIVER

If the Tree of life keeps both sides of the River of Life, then there must be two character traits to the Tree of Life. So, let us look into the Word of God to see if we can find those two traits:

Proverbs 3:13-18

> *Happy is the man that findeth wisdom, and the man that getteth understanding. For the merchandise of it is better than the merchandise of silver, and the gain thereof than fine gold. She is more precious than rubies: and all the things thou canst desire are not to be compared unto her.*
>
> *Length of days is in her right hand; and in her left hand riches and honour. Her ways are ways of pleasantness, and all her paths are peace. She is a tree of life to them that lay hold upon her: and happy is every one that retaineth her.*

Wisdom is a Tree of Life. By her, you can have long days, riches, and honor. You can know if it is wisdom because her instructions will be pleasant in the way it tells you to respond. Wisdom will always lead to the path of peace. Wisdom is the takeaway from each season of your life. Learning what the Holy Spirit has to teach you in every one of life's turns will keep you firmly in the River of Life.

Maybe that is what John meant in 1 John 2:20 when he said, *"But ye have an unction from the Holy One, and ye know all things."*

In another of the Proverbs, we find:

Proverbs 11:30

> *The fruit of the righteous is a tree of life; and he that winneth souls is wise.*

The fruit that living righteously develops in your life will lead you to the Tree of Life. The righteousness that comes from the Tree of Life is defined here as a life that leads people to Jesus, or, we could say, a life that leads people to their tribe. So when we live in a way that everything about us points to who and what we believe in, it will keep us in the River of Life.

So, we can see how the two things the Word says about the Tree of Life keep the two banks of the river.

Ezekiel had a lot to say about both the River of Life and the Tree of Life:

Ezekiel 47:6-9

> *And he said unto me, Son of man, hast thou seen this? Then he brought me, and caused me to return to the brink of the river. Now when I had returned, behold, at the bank of the river were very many trees on the one side and on the other. Then said he unto me, These waters issue out toward the east country, and go down into the desert, and go into the sea: which being brought forth into the sea, the waters shall be healed. And it shall come to pass, that every thing that liveth, which moveth, whithersoever the rivers shall come, shall live: and there shall be a very great multitude of fish, because these waters shall come thither: for they shall be healed; and every thing shall live whither the river cometh.*

I want to note here that Ezekiel saw many trees holding the bank. (I will come back to this a little later.) The river is to bring life and health to everything it touches. Jesus said that the river is in us:

John 7:38

He that believeth on me, as the scripture hath said, out of his belly shall flow rivers of living water.

Ezekiel had more to say about the river:

Ezekiel 47:10-12

And it shall come to pass, that the fishers shall stand upon it from Engedi even unto Eneglaim; they shall be a place to spread forth nets; their fish shall be according to their kinds, as the fish of the great sea, exceeding many. But the miry places thereof and the marishes thereof shall not be healed; they shall be given to salt. And by the river upon the bank thereof, on this side and on that side, shall grow all trees for meat, whose leaf shall not fade, neither shall the fruit thereof be consumed: it shall bring forth new fruit according to his months, because their waters they issued out of the sanctuary: and the fruit thereof shall be for meat, and the leaf thereof for medicine.

The harvest from the river is from Engedi, which means "a fountain of a kid," or "from your youth," to Eneglaim, which means "a fountain of a full grown calf," or "from your maturity." This is indicating the lessons you learn from youth through the rest of life. It looks like the river and the trees work together to bring us to all Jesus has for us.

Notice that these trees bring forth fruit according to the season, just like the Tree of Life. And their leaves are for healing, just like the Tree of Life. So it sounds like the Tree of Life has multiplied itself, and indeed it has. If the river flows out of the sanctuary, then the river and the tree live inside of us.

Remember, Jesus said, *"Behold, the kingdom of God is within you"* (Luke 17:21). This is very, very important, and you should stop here and give God glory for all He is doing inside of you! I want to emphasize that: because the Tree of Life is in you, those around you are kept in the river.

THE RIVER OF LIFE

Now, let's go back to the garden and this time let's look at the River of Life:

Genesis 2:8-10

And the LORD God planted a garden eastward in Eden; and there he put the man whom he had formed. And out of the ground made the LORD God to grow every tree that is pleasant to the sight, and good for food; the tree of life also in the midst of the garden, and the tree of knowledge of good and evil. And a river went out of Eden to water the garden; and from thence it was parted, and became into four heads.

One river parts and becomes four tributaries that we can drink from. Each tributary has a different gift from God to bring us to the fullness of His life. Let's examine one tributary at a time and see what Jesus has for us:

PISON

Genesis 2:11-12

The name of the first is Pison: that is it which compasseth the whole land of Havilah, where there is gold; and the gold of that land is good: there is bdellium and the onyx stone.

Wow! Would you like to find this place? It is a place full of good gold and rare, costly stones. I believe the gold speaks of God's glory and the stones of His increase. So whatever it is that we get from drinking from Pison, it will lead us into the glory of God and His increase in our lives.

Pison in the original Hebrew text was *pee-shone,* which comes from the root word *poosh,* meaning "to grow up." The first of the tributaries is a place of growing up. We have to grow up in some things to walk in God's glory and His increase. If you have trouble encountering God's glory, maybe there is some growing up you need to do. The more you learn to live the Kingdom life (as defined by the Word of God), the more of His glory you will encounter.

As my friend Joshua Mills says, "It is not if you are comfortable with the glory, but is the glory comfortable with you." On the same note, if you are not enjoying God's increase in your life, you may need to grow up in tithing and giving. To walk in God's blessings, you have to follow His plan of increase. You may need to grow up in money management skills. You may need a Dave Ramsey's Financial Peace type class to teach you the needed skill-sets about managing money.

I think it is noteworthy that Pison is in the land of Havilah, which comes from the root word *khool*, which means "a place of pain." Growing up is not always a fun thing. But, as you spend time growing up in the ways of the Kingdom of God, you will find yourself at the second tributary, Gihon.

GIHON

Genesis 2:13

> *And the name of the second river is Gihon: the same is it that compasseth the whole land of Ethiopia.*

Gihon is from the root word *ghee'-akh*, which means "to break forth" or "break out." After we have grown up some in the Lord, it is time to break out of those things that keep us from all God has for us, things that have been passed down from generation to generation.

Some of these things are learned behaviors. You may be repeating things you observed others doing. You may need a freedom *SOZO*-type class to help you at this part of the river.

You may even need to go back and drink from Pison, to do some more growing up. Repeat it as often as needed. This will help you get all that Gihon has for you.

Gihon is a place of letting go of *you* and holding on to Jesus. The more you are willing to deal with the learned behaviors in your life, the more Jesus can teach you His Kingdom behaviors. This will help you be prepared for the next tributary, Hiddekel.

HIDDEKEL

Genesis 2:14

And the name of the third river is Hiddekel: that is it which goeth toward the east of Assyria.

Hiddekel means "rapid growth." So when we have drunk from Gihon, we will experience times of rapid growth. Those learned behaviors that we hold as truth could be the very thing holding us back from this rapid growth.

Hiddekel is an amazing stream to drink from, but, first, you have to already have drunk from the other tributaries to get here.

So, again, if you find yourselves in a place of no growth, you may need to go back to Pison to do some more growing up. Then, back to Gihon to get some breakthroughs, so that Jesus can then release another quick work in you.

Congratulations! You have reached the final stream, Euphrates.

EUPHRATES

Genesis 2:14

And the fourth river is Euphrates.

The word Euphrates is translated from the Hebrew *per-awth'*, from an unused root, meaning "to break forth." When all four tributaries are at work in our lives, we break forth and become a place of fruitfulness. We become a resource for all of those around us.

The life lessons we learned at Pison, the break out we got at Gihon, and the growth we experienced at Hiddekel all become resources we can offer to others. If we begin to turn those resources (like wisdom or increase) inward and use them only for ourselves, we will find ourselves no longer able to drink from Euphrates. Euphrates is where you become a leader who builds the Body of Jesus, and only leaders get to continue to drink from this stream.

STAY IN THE GARDEN

And now, for my final thoughts on the garden of God. Genesis 2 shows us:

Genesis 2:15-18

> And the LORD God took the man, and put him into the garden of Eden to dress it and to keep it. And the LORD God commanded the man, saying, Of every tree of the garden thou mayest freely eat: but of the tree of the knowledge of good and evil, thou shalt not eat of it: for in the day that thou eatest thereof thou shalt surely die. And the LORD God said, It is not good that the man should be alone; I will make him an help meet for him.

You and I were originally created to live in the garden, to dress and keep it. It is the place where we learn to serve the Lord and His Kingdom. Every tree that is good for us is there. But the tree of disobedience is there as well. It is also the place we learn to obey God.

Last, but not least, I get a help meet there, that perfect someone who will come alongside me and complete me in my journey through a perfect union of marriage. This union needs every part of the river to be made whole. It is only by living in the garden that I am equipped with all I need to walk in the fullness that Jesus has for me.

I want to reiterate what I said in the beginning of this chapter. Living in the Garden will bring us to our highest potential, both in our physical life and in our walk in the Kingdom of God. There's no place that can compare with the Garden of God. Will you join me in the Garden?

Author Contact Page

You may contact Kim Voisin in the following ways:

Pastor Kim F. Voisin
Vision Christian Center
4467 Hwy 24, Bourg, LA 70343

Phone: 985.594.8888